Home Inspection Secrets of a Happy Home Inspector

A Guide to Peace of Mind for

Home Buyers, Sellers, and the Agents

who Love Them

By Wally Conway

Disclaimer: This book is designed to provide information on the home inspection profession and the home inspector's role in the real estate transaction. It is intended to assist buyers, sellers, agents, lenders, lawyers, and home inspectors in understanding the issues involved in blending the inspector's input into decisions about the transaction.

It is not the purpose of this manual to reprint or restate all the information that is otherwise available from other authors, publishers, or governmental agencies. Rather, it is intended to complement, amplify, and supplement other texts. You are urged to read all available material, learn as much as possible about the subject, and tailor information to your specific needs.

Home inspection has become a sophisticated profession. No part of it is a get-rich-quick scheme. In addition to reading this book, anyone who desires to become a home inspector should do much additional research to avoid harming themselves or others.

Every effort has been made to write a book that is as complete and accurate as possible. However, there may be mistakes, both typographical and in content. Therefore, this book should be used only as a guide and thought-provoking mechanism. All referenced experience and knowledge is specific to the state of Florida, unless stated otherwise. Your location may be different in many or all aspects.

Please note that credentials and experience matters. An inspector simply stating that they are "certified" or "licensed" really does not mean very much. You must study the license requirements for your state and certification requirements of professional organizations before making the choice to hire or refer a home inspector.

The purpose of this book is to educate and entertain; no representations or warranties are made with respect to completeness or accuracy of its contents. The author and publisher shall have neither liability nor responsibility to any person or entity with respect to any loss or damage caused, or alleged to have been caused, directly or indirectly, by the information contained in this book. Further, readers should be aware that the Internet websites listed in this work may have changed or disappeared between the time this work was written and when it is read.

Author's Note

Writing for me has been a great challenge. The only way I could get through this was to simply write my experiences and explain how they have shaped my ideas about the profession of home inspecting. Thoughts expressed here are a greatest hits compendium of my time spent inspecting houses since 1994. If an anecdote sounds like it is about you and you enjoy it, you are welcome to savor it. But if you think it is about you and you are sad, it is not about you!

"If you're not having fun doing your thing, you're either doing the wrong thing, or your thing wrong".

-- Wally Conway

Dedication

To all the soldiers, sailors, airmen, and marines who have lost their lives defending a place we call home.

To my Naval Academy roommate, Capt. Stephen J. Burley, USMC.

To my USS Saratoga (CV-62) shipmate, Capt. Michael S. Speicher, USN.

Faces of fallen friends are never forgotten.

TABLE OF CONTENTS

A Free Bonus Before We Begin

A Few Brief But Important Acknowledgements

Who is this guy Wally Conway?

Additional Resources – Wally's Coming to Your Town!

It's No Secret What People Are Saying About Wally's Way!

Chapter 1: What's This Book About?

Chapter 2: What is the Secret to Success and Happiness in Real Estate?

Chapter 3: Confessions of a Contract Assassin!

Chapter 4: What Qualifies a Home Inspector You Can Trust?

Chapter 5 - How Should a Home Be Judged?

Chapter 6 - Why Do Assassins Have Contracts?

Chapter 7 - What If You Had a Party and Nobody Came?

Chapter 8 - Can You Find Reality in a Home Inspection Report?

Chapter 9 - The Truth about Agents Referring Home Inspectors

Chapter 10 - Secrets to Reducing Risk and Delay in Real Estate Repairs

Chapter 11 - Why Do We Need Home Inspectors When We Have Building Departments?

Chapter 12 - Is This a Home Inspection or Crime Scene Investigation?

Chapter 13 - Should Brand New Homes be Inspected?

Chapter 14 - And in Closing I'd Like to Say......

information about the transaction. Another goal of buyers and sellers should be to involve those professionals along the path of the transaction that will aid in keeping surprise at bay. The goal of each professional participating along the way should be to educate buyers and sellers to minimize the surprise in each and every facet of the transaction.

Since houses come in many shapes, sizes, ages, and price ranges, how are we to remove the surprise element? And, by the way, buyers and sellers come in even more varieties than houses! What IS a professional to do?

Managing Expectations

The simplest approach to keeping people happy is to manage their expectations. Manage the expectations of the transaction in its ENTIRETY! The expectations of the home itself are daunting enough, but to then manage the reasonable performance expectations of the various and varied participants in the transaction is truly a challenge. But, by peeking at each element individually brings clarity to the challenge of managing expectations.

During live seminars, I often give an interactive example of managing expectations. I set up the scenario explaining that it is just a play. It goes something like this:

"Ma'am, I am in town for a short period of time, and do not enjoy dining alone. Would you give me the favor of your company for lunch?"

Understand at this point that the person chosen is always someone whom I have never met. Another point to make is that as the guest presenter, I am always well-dressed and well-spoken. In the mind of the lady chosen for lunch, I am also well paid, so she expects that we will be dining in fine fashion.

The lunch lady then responds, "Yes, I would be happy to accompany you to lunch".

The truth of the matter is – her expectations for lunch and my intentions for lunch are vastly different!

I go on to explain to the class. After my speaking engagements, I usually either drive myself to the airport or back home. It has become a ritual of

TABLE OF CONTENTS

A Free Bonus Before We Begin

A Few Brief But Important Acknowledgements

Who is this guy Wally Conway?

Additional Resources – Wally's Coming to Your Town!

It's No Secret What People Are Saying About Wally's Way!

Chapter 1: What's This Book About?

Chapter 2: What is the Secret to Success and Happiness in Real Estate?

Chapter 3: Confessions of a Contract Assassin!

Chapter 4: What Qualifies a Home Inspector You Can Trust?

Chapter 5 - How Should a Home Be Judged?

Chapter 6 - Why Do Assassins Have Contracts?

Chapter 7 - What If You Had a Party and Nobody Came?

Chapter 8 - Can You Find Reality in a Home Inspection Report?

Chapter 9 - The Truth about Agents Referring Home Inspectors

Chapter 10 - Secrets to Reducing Risk and Delay in Real Estate Repairs

Chapter 11 - Why Do We Need Home Inspectors When We Have Building Departments?

Chapter 12 - Is This a Home Inspection or Crime Scene Investigation?

Chapter 13 - Should Brand New Homes be Inspected?

Chapter 14 - And in Closing I'd Like to Say……

A Free Bonus Before We Begin

Would you like to know HOW to make great decisions when choosing a home inspector?

There are secrets in the home inspection business, and some of them are dirty secrets. Most home inspectors don't want these secrets revealed, because keeping their secrets is what keeps them in business. By asking the right questions, you can be protected.

My special 28-page report "The Dirty Dozen Secrets that Other Home Inspectors Don't Want You to Know" is available to you as a free bonus for purchasing this book. Just visit www.GetAHomeInspector.com

A Few Brief But Important Acknowledgements

Those experienced in the ways of publishing would suggest that acknowledgements are intended to be at the end of the book. They are to be used as a thank you to those of influence that created the experiences that led to sparks that became this book. Maybe there's good reason there is an established precedent. But I choose a different path.

Drawing on the lessons of Steven Covey in *The 7 Habits of Highly Effective People*, and with great respect for Dr. Covey, blending Habit #2 "Begin with the end in mind", with a backwards twist on Habit #5 "Seek first to understand, then to be understood", my intent in placing the acknowledgements in the front to the book is to give you some insight into how I got here and where we are going together in the book.

This was actually the last part of this book left for me to write. As it turns out, I saved the toughest task for last. When you really get down to it, by the time you've gained enough experience to write a business book, you have to thank everyone from your parents to whoever was on the phone as you keyed the last stroke!

That leaves only two choices. Create a separate tome of acknowledgments, or leave someone out.

With no ill-will intended, I have gone the short route for simplicity. To those unacknowledged, I truly thank you and appreciate your contributions to this book and to my life.

My saga as a home inspector began back in 1994. As I was about to retire from a career as a Navy Pilot I was searching for a new career that would replace the challenges of flying off aircraft carriers. I had earned a contractor's license back in 1986 and had a great interest as well as some experience with renovation and real estate investing.

Home inspection was a relatively young profession in 1994, but it seemed like a good idea at the time. As I write this some twenty years and 30,000 home inspections later, it was a good decision.

Along the way I've been privileged with opportunities in radio and television. I've done over 20 episodes of *House Detective* on Home and Garden Television (HGTV) and co-hosted DIY Network's *Finders Fixers*. In

2003, I jumped into radio – my original show has morphed over the years but is still going strong today as *The Home and Garden Show* on WOKV. Life has been very, very good!

The good fortune that has come to my home inspection company, HomePro Inspections, did not come fast, nor did it come by my efforts alone. Many of my peers have confessed to me in private that they are envious of the fabulous group of inspectors and staff that work with me at HomePro Inspections. They are the reason that I have been able to take on the task of doing all the seminars, television, radio, and writing!

Someone working alone could have done none of what I've done. I have been surrounded by the best and brightest since the beginning, and they have allowed me the flexibility to truly live this business to its fullest.

The first on board was Bob Wagner way back in 1995. Why he made the decision to work with some nut running a business out of his van, I will never understand, but he worked with me steadily, day in and day out, until his retirement. We worked together over 15 years, and I wish him all the best!

Another person in early was Chris Brown. How a Model "A" collector and old house remodeler came to work with Bob and me, a couple of retired Navy fliers, is beyond me, but through thick, thin, and thousands of inspections, Chris was the greatest. Chris also chose retirement a couple years ago – in North Carolina, no less! I've had other great guys, but these are the guys who really got it going and who provided training to many who followed.

Speaking of my team, I enjoy and respect them so much that each is featured prominently on the HomePro website. Each has established a legion of satisfied customers and a loyal referral base.

From the beginning we have been focused at making every member of the HomePro team as productive as possible as fast as possible. Take a peek at www.GoHomePro.com. They argue over who is the most handsome. Your input is welcome! And we are always interested in adding new team members!

My wife Tonya is amazing. I am a guy who is constantly thinking, constantly dreaming up new things to do with the company, but the truth is my detail skills would not get me too far. I make a lot of messes! Tonya is one of those rare and wonderful people who gets excited about bringing order to the chaos created by others. I excel at creating chaos. I am forever thankful that she forgives me my imperfections.

I am truly thankful for each of you has as encouraged and enabled the joy and success that I have experienced and continue to experience in my life. May we all live long and prosper!

Who is this guy Wally Conway?

Wally has been featured on the Home and Garden Television (HGTV) series *House Detective*, co-hosted *Finders Fixers* on the DIY Network, and hosts a weekly radio show on WOKV in Jacksonville called *The Home and Garden Show*. He is also a frequent contributor to an assortment of magazines, newsletters and television news programs.

He is President of Florida HomePro Inc. (HomePro Inspections), the home inspection company he founded in 1994. Beginning as a sole practitioner, the business evolved rapidly to become one of the largest independently-owned multi-inspector firms in Florida. In addition, Wally serves as a respected consultant to many other home inspection companies. A retired Navy pilot and a graduate of the U. S. Naval Academy, he became a Florida licensed residential contractor in 1986.

As a specialist in discovery, disclosure, and documentation of residential concerns, Wally has authored and instructed numerous courses approved by the Florida Real Estate Commission (FREC) for the continuing education of real estate agents. Standard course topics cover home inspection and construction related issues. Wally has educated literally thousands of REALTORS® on the specifics needed to comply with state statutes, as well as how to comfort buyers and sellers during the tense time of a real estate transaction while simultaneously managing agent interest and liability.

Wally has been a staff instructor with the Florida Association of REALTORS® Instructor Academy. He is steadily involved with the Northeast Florida Association of REALTORS® (NEFAR), having participated on the Legislative Committee and the Education Committee over many years. NEFAR's Education program won the state's highest honor, the Outstanding Education Programs Award, during his tenure as Chairman.

Wally has served as the President of the Florida Chapter of the American Society of Home Inspectors (FLASHI), on the board of the Florida Association of Building Inspectors (FABI), as a member of the ASHI Council of Representatives, as a member of the ASHI Strategic Planning Committee, and is a Member of InterNACHI.

Wally interacts regularly with a wide-ranging client base including residential and commercial building buyers, sellers, property managers, renovators, investors, lenders, agents, attorneys, appraisers, and their frequent satisfied referrals. He has received numerous honors and much recognition for his outstanding service. Among those awards is Northeast Florida Association of REALTORS® Affiliate of the Year!

Additional Resources – Wally's Coming to Your Town!

No matter how hard I have tried, I just can't get all that I want to share with you into this book. And the biggest bummer to writing is that I'm not getting to hear your thoughts as you read!

It would be great fun to do some things together. Just a sampling of what we could do is described below. As you ponder my proposals to follow, something is going to come to you that seems like a fun fit.

The really fun thing is that as you read on you might have an idea that I forgot to mention or one that I've never even thought of. Those are really the exciting ones.

We should do something fun together, here are just few ideas to get us started:

TV would be great fun. Having done HGTV for a few years I got the bug to produce a show. No to be type cast as just a house guy, this show was about a couple of buddies who loved boats, you can sneak a peak of the show format at www.MyBuddiesBoat.com. Next TV production was back into houses with the development of a program about reducing energy expenses at home, which was tons of fun.

We could do radio together! The first foray into radio was over a decade ago with The Happy Home Inspector Show, which has since morphed into The Home and Garden Show heard every Saturday on NewsTalk WOKV. You can listen live or via podcast at www.WOKV.com.

Radio has been great fun and an exceptional business builder by creating a simultaneous position of credibility and celebrity. For years it has confounded me that every small business owner or entrepreneur does not host a local radio show. After having hundreds of people tell me they would love to have their own radio show, but just didn't know I created a program to teach you how to do it yourself! Interested?

Doing live seminars got my business off the ground. What started as one-on-one presentations to real estate agents in open houses grew to a seminar business that has allowed me to present at hundreds of events and venues from local Jacksonville market to national events in the US and Canada, even on cruise ships! Want to work together at upcoming event, yours or mine? www.WallyConway.com

If you don't want to deal with travel, then webinars and teleseminars are the ticket – faster, more flexible, and easier to produce. Doing a program together from a distance might a perfect first experience together! And the cool thing about these programs is that they put us on a path to podcast. Been there yet?

Interviews and articles are also great way to get to know each other. Heck, we could even write a book!

In truth, there is no media or method that can't be used effectively to deliver great content. We've got a ton of content plus the breadth of production experience to deliver what's needed – when and where it's needed. And as I often say, I'm available for international travel.

To find out more or to explore an idea, email me directly at wally@wallyconway.com call 800-270-9791.

It's No Secret What People Say About Wally's Way!

Your company is the best! I live in Chicago but was having a home inspected in Florida, and Tonya and Amie did a great job of emailing me the documents and answering all my questions. They were terrific as first line contacts with your company. The inspector was incredible too; he explained everything he was doing, answered my many questions, and I will recommend him highly. Everyone was very professional and nice. Can't recommend you highly enough! -- Karin Kinzalow (Home Buyer)

For more than 20 years, I have recommended HomePro to my buyers. All have been very satisfied with the inspection team. Both of our daughters have used HomePro inspections, too. Can't believe there are any buyers out there that are more hard to please than them. Wally, you are the best! Thanks for all you and your team do to make my real estate life easy. Babs Bowler (REALTOR)

HomePro Inspections came to my house and showed me several ways I could save on my energy spending for very little upfront cost. I did most of the work myself. Tom Goldsbury (Homeowner)

We had a very complicated home inspection with an historic house over 100 years old. It took more than one trip for the inspector as we had to get power, water, and gas turned on and, of course, it did not go as expected. The inspector was very knowledgeable and helpful, both during and after the inspection. I had several follow-up questions for him which we handled via email after his visits. He was timely and considerate. I would recommend these folks for sure. Sabra Morgan (Home Buyer)

Our parish was considering a purchase of a large school building that had not been used for five years. When I contacted local real estate companies about inspectors the name Home Pro kept coming up, and especially Wally's name. After we contacted Wally, we soon learned why; he was accurate in his assessment, honest about worth and the future needs of the building and his candid manner quickly earned our trust. I would recommend this company to anyone or any organization. Tom Hable (Property Manager)

I can only say good things about Home Pro. They are professional, friendly and most importantly very knowledgeable in what they do. I would recommend them to anyone looking to have an inspection done. Art Borde (Home Buyer)

As a Realtor I only recommend companies I have confidence in and HomePro is one of those. Austin Barbour has done many inspections for my customers over the years & I highly recommend him as an inspector. Thank you HomePro! Ann Abercrombie (REALTOR)

I live in Minnesota and needed a home inspected in Florida. Home Pro was recommended to me and they did a great job! They coordinated an appointment time with my realtor and sent me a very thorough report. I would recommend them to everyone. Thank you for a professional job! Patti Timm (Home Buyer)

HomePro is terrific with home inspections. Every nook and cranny, every room, floor, wall, ceiling, light fixture, and anything else affixed was thoroughly checked to be sure it functions properly. Computer reports were well written, easy to read and understand, and photos to inform buyer about situations. Great inspectors, great service, very thorough, great working with them. Amy Lipper (REALTOR)

During the home buying process, it is always a concern that there are hidden problems. 17 years ago, we used the HomePro team and the information at that time was very helpful. So when I found myself a single woman, looking to purchase my first home alone, I contacted them again. HomePro sent a top notch professional to inspect my purchase. He answered all my questions, to exasperation, I'm afraid, and was incredible helpful making sure I understood everything. I highly recommend the HomePro Inspection team, and would use them again in a heartbeat. Karen Burgess (Home Buyer)

I knew that my customer and I were going to get the best service possible and actually at an affordable price for the work that was done. Your inspector checked and documented everything. What was great was the infrared work he did. I think that's just the best, especially in some of these units that have been slapped and painted for quick move in. You really need to know what's behind the walls! Sondra Sparapani (REALTOR)

Amazing experience! The Home Pro Team was very professional and very detailed. They were able to show me things about the house that I never would have thought of. They were very patient with my questions, and took the time to personally show me every warning sign or problem that they found. The infrared camera was awesome! Also had a great list of trusted professionals that could assist me on any future project. I am very confident with the service provided. The 5 Star Package I would highly recommend to anyone that might be buying a house. It might be a little more expensive than some other local inspectors but the money saved is well worth it. I won't trust one of the largest investments in my life to anyone else. Thank you Home Pro! Rating: 5 Stars -- Patrick Sullivan (Home Buyer)

I always use HomePro, precise and through inspections and reports for me and my clients. Always arrive on time and are very professional in demeanor and appearance. Pam Nall-Haskett (REALTOR)

My HomePro experience was excellent. Your company personnel are professional, personable and a pleasure to work with. It is one of the few times that people have done exactly what they said they would do when they said they would do it and in the most professional way possible. I cannot thank you enough for conducting a thorough inspection and uncovering areas of concern that had the potential to make this home a true 'money pit'. While we have decided not to purchase this home, we would wholeheartedly recommend your service to anyone considering a home purchase. Our realtor tried to steer us away from using your service by inferring that you were the 'most expensive'. I don't know whether or not this is true, but from my perspective your service is worth the fee and when we find the 'right' home we will once again use your inspection service. Please do not hesitate to use my name as a referral for your service. Thank you for a job well done, MaryAnne Williams (Home Buyer)

CHAPTER 1
What's This Book About?

The label "Deal Killer" seems to have been stamped on home inspectors the same day that the first contractor laid down his tools and announced that he was a home inspector.

Back in the dark ages of the 1970s, the home inspector's mantra was "I can find something wrong with every home". And they did. And it is good to find fault where there is fault. But faults are not the only facts that are needed to fairly and objectively describe a home.

All this negative talk scared home buyers, insulted home sellers, and enraged real estate agents. Real estate deals that would have closed with the buyer living happily ever after were dying like never before. These early home inspector fellows were truly "Deal Killers".

Meanwhile, our friends down under in Australia were also having a tough time with their own home inspectors. The Aussies, though, are a bit more refined then we Americans in some ways, yet they possess a cowboy-like defiance for authority. It was the real estate agents of Australia who coined the term "Contract Assassin" in response to the number of real estate contracts that were killed by home inspectors.

Contract Assassin!

Not what my mother hoped I would grow up to be, but compelling nonetheless.

Deal Killer!

Again, nothing to brag about.

Why would such hostile terms be used to describe a profession as well-intended as home inspection? What perspective needs to be shared so that home inspectors can be seen as comforters of anxious buyers and contract confirmers?

That is where we are going together. Buyer, seller, agent, lender, appraiser, lawyer, and inspector—we all travel together to get to where we are going. And where ARE we going? We're going to get the deal done, and done for the good of all, different as their agendas may be.

It is unlikely that we will agree on every point, but it is critical that we address every issue. Writing has not changed my thoughts on any aspect of the home inspection process, but it has necessitated a dissecting of how and why I came to the business belief system that I have.

My hope is that I have been able to express thoughts clearly enough and succinctly enough that we will agree on most issues. As for those issues on which we differ, my hope is that we be able to respect each other and our differing opinions.

CHAPTER 2
What is the Secret to Success and Happiness
in Real Estate?

What is it that makes us happy? If you got this book from the self-help section, it was in the wrong place! But while we're on the subject of happiness, let's continue.

People want to be happy with their home purchase. They want to be happy with their home sale, be happy with their agent, appraiser, lender, lawyer, and even with their home inspector! So how is it that people become happy?

No Good Surprises

Having now been involved in over 25,000 real estate transactions, it has come to my attention that there are no good surprises in real estate. Surprisingly enough, not once has a buyer ever called my office to say that, to their great and happy surprise, the home has more bedrooms than what was told to them by their agent!

Not once has a buyer called with delight to share that while mowing the lawn for the first time they discovered an unexpected but crystal clear swimming pool!

And not even once has someone called to announce that upon the first opening of the garage, low and behold, a free Ferrari!

Nope, wish as we will, surprises in real estate are always bad. Back to those 25,000 deals. Having observed and pondered at length who is happy and who is sad, I have come to the conclusion that people are happy when things turn out as well or better than expected; not necessarily that they turned out well! People simply hate surprises in real estate.

Since it is true that people hate surprises in real estate, then each person involved in the real estate transaction should be given clear specifications of how to avoid surprises!

The first goal of buyers and sellers should be to bring to bear all information about the transaction. Another goal of buyers and sellers should be to involve those professionals along the path of the transaction that will aid in keeping surprise at bay. The goal of each professional participating along the way should be to educate buyers and sellers to minimize the surprise in each and every facet of the transaction.

Since houses come in many shapes, sizes, ages, and price ranges, how are we to remove the surprise element? And, by the way, buyers and sellers come in even more varieties than houses! What IS a professional to do?

Managing Expectations

The simplest approach to keeping people happy is to manage their expectations. Manage the expectations of the transaction in its ENTIRETY! The expectations of the home itself are daunting enough, but to then manage the reasonable performance expectations of the various and varied participants in the transaction is truly a challenge. But, by peeking at each element individually brings clarity to the challenge of managing expectations.

During live seminars, I often give an interactive example of managing expectations. I set up the scenario explaining that it is just a play. It goes something like this:

"Ma'am, I am in town for a short period of time, and do not enjoy dining alone. Would you give me the favor of your company for lunch?"

Understand at this point that the person chosen is always someone whom I have never met. Another point to make is that as the guest presenter, I am always well-dressed and well-spoken. In the mind of the lady chosen for lunch, I am also well paid, so she expects that we will be dining in fine fashion.

The lunch lady then responds, "Yes, I would be happy to accompany you to lunch".

The truth of the matter is – her expectations for lunch and my intentions for lunch are vastly different!

I go on to explain to the class. After my speaking engagements, I usually either drive myself to the airport or back home. It has become a ritual of mine to seek out a hotdog joint after speaking. I have no idea why this is; it is just what I do! The dialog continues as though we are at lunch and about to order:

"Ma'am, would you like chili or sauerkraut on your hotdog?"

The look on the woman's face is always the same. It is a blend of shock and disappointment. She had visions of something fancy-schmancy; I had visions of chili, onions, and mustard dripping down my chin!

Her expectations were not met.

But, had her expectations been properly managed, it could have been a great time at the dog shack! What if the dialog had been:

"Ma'am, it is a road ritual of mine to find the best hotdog joint in town after every seminar. If you give me your best suggestion, I'll buy you the dog of your choice!"

Now, fully informed, expectations fully managed, off we go to enjoy our hotdogs. And we are darn thrilled about it!

That is the art of managing expectations. That is the duty of the real estate agent.

Another Thing Mom Never Told You

When someone buys a home, they purchase 100 percent of the home. They seek to use 100 percent of the home 100 percent of the time. They want the entire house to be available to them all of the time. But somehow, there is a denial of the risks associated with home ownership.

When you own 100 percent of the home, you also own 100 percent of the RISK.

The best way to manage risk is to first recognize that there IS risk. Then take steps that are reasonable and rational to identify specific risk. Some people think that the service providers present in a real estate transaction are there just to take their money. Au contraire! (That's a fancy way of saying "on the contrary"). Those service providers are actually there to help buyers identify and manage their RISK in the transaction.

Everyone would like to eliminate the risks. While it may be impossible or unduly expensive to eliminate ALL the risks, a look at some simple risk reduction tools can greatly help in understanding buyer risk.

Agents as Risk Reducers

The initial risk reduction tool employed by most home buyers is the use of a real estate agent. In the hands of an experienced professional providing expert guidance, many risks can be exposed or eliminated. The trail is always safer with an experienced trail guide! The real estate agent has traveled the trail many times before and often has a clear picture of the hazards along the way.

Appraise the Risks

Appraisers can also reduce some of the risk. The risk reduction provided by the appraiser is a determination of the home's fair market value. If the home buyer were to overpay for a property, that overpayment is money at risk. In the event that the property needed to be returned to the market, it is unlikely that it could be sold at a price above the fair market value. The amount of the overpayment would be lost. The appraiser can reduce that risk.

Survey the Risks

The land surveyor can further reduce the home buyer's risk. The surveyor will confirm that the property is of the size and dimension represented. On a typical survey, all buildings on the property will be depicted, as well as the position of fences, sheds, and driveways. Setbacks and easements that might affect present and future use will be identified, as well as any flood zones.

It is amazing how many homeowners have unknowingly built fences, sheds, or driveways on a neighbor's property without problem or issue until one of the properties is sold. The land surveyor can reduce the home buyer's risk.

Fund the Risks

The lender also reduces the home buyer's risk. Lenders are absolute experts at reducing their own risk, and in the process, many of the benefits of the lender's risk reduction are transferred to the home buyer. The mandatory inspections and verifications that the lender requires to reduce the likelihood of the home buyer defaulting on the mortgage and forcing foreclosure ensure that if the home is destroyed, the home buyer is also protected. Lenders can reduce the home buyer's risk.

The Legal Risks

Lawyers can reduce home buyers' risk. The pile of paper needed to purchase a home can be perplexing and frustrating! It is critical that every document be complete and accurate to ensure that ownership is conveyed correctly to the new owner. A slip in any detail of the paperwork can have untold consequences that might not show themselves for years or decades to come. On occasion, these flaws are not discovered until the homeowner is deceased and the heirs are attempting to clear probate. We may not live forever, but the paper trail is eternal and must be correct. Lawyers can reduce the risk of home ownership.

Title Risks

Title companies can reduce the risk of home ownership. Over the decades, parcels of land may have changed ownership dozens of times. Large parcels are subdivided to make neighborhoods. Often, multiple heirs have had claim to land that has long been forgotten. Mortgage notes and taxes due are sometimes abandoned. But when the property is sold or transferred, old debts and demons often rise.

The title company can discover this past and prevent this cloud from hanging over the parcel and the person forever. And for an additional fee, the title company can insure against any missed issue or future claim against your clear title to the property. Title companies can reduce the risk of home ownership.

Insure the Risks

Insurance companies can reduce the risk of home ownership. Principally though the writing of homeowner's insurance policies, insurance companies reduce the financial risk to homeowners.

These policies work in two basic areas—peril and liability. Peril would be fire, flood, theft, or similar threats to the property. Liability reduction includes provisions of payment to an injured or otherwise harmed individual when some unfortunate circumstance occurs in or around your home. Insurance companies can reduce the risk of home ownership.

Bond the Risks

Termite bonding companies can reduce the risk of home ownership. Termites do more damage to homes each year then fire and flood combined. In many areas of the country the question is not if your home will have termites, just when. Termite bonding companies will treat affected areas or repair damage to your home should a termite infestation occur. Termite bonding companies can reduce the risk of home ownership

Warrant the Risks

Home warranty companies can reduce the risk of home ownership. There will always be unforeseen failures of the systems and components of your home. Preparing for many of these unwanted and unpredictable expenses can be done with a home warranty policy. These types of policies act to protect appliance and system failures not typically protected by homeowners' insurance policies. Though home warranties do not cover every eventuality, they can reduce the risk of home ownership.

Inspect the Risks

Home inspections can reduce the risk of home ownership. The role of the home inspector in risk reduction is to search for signs, symptoms, and clues that would indicate some damage or defect may be located within the home. By ascertaining risk that is discoverable prior to the purchase of the home, issues affecting performance, maintenance, and/or value can be addressed. In some instances, the defects discovered are of sufficient magnitude to eliminate the desire to own the home. Home inspectors can reduce the risk of home ownership.

A Home with a Side of Risk

When it is all said and done, we simply do not want risk! We do not want risk with such passion that real risks are routinely ignored and denied. Don't put your head in the sand!

I said it earlier, and I'll say it again: the best way to manage risk is to first recognize that there IS risk. Then take steps that are reasonable and rational to identify specific risk. Home inspectors, surveyors, and title searchers all aid in risk identification. These professionals identify risk in exchange for a fee.

With risks identified, we can begin risk reduction or transfer. The insurance, warranty, and termite bonding companies handle risk reduction and transfer responsibilities. These companies accept risk from the homeowner in exchange for a fee.

This entire process is about exchanging some amount of money for the identification and reassignment of risk to some entity other than the homeowner. The idea is to spend a known amount to preclude the loss of an unknown or potentially unlimited amount. That, ladies and gentlemen, is risk management in the home buying process.

Bringing Reason to Risk

So why the diatribe on risk? In having spoken to thousands of real estate agents and home buyers alike, I have found that when the concepts of risk and risk management are explained, most get it and agree both on how to handle it and who is ultimately responsible for assuming the risks.

To be sure you get it, I'll say it differently. The homeowner who owns the home likewise owns the risk. To get risk to the smallest amount possible, we first take the whole bundle of risk, and then go about identifying and handing off small pieces of that risk in exchange for small fees. It's just like cutting a cake!

After this process, the homeowner is left with a smaller pile of risk. The homeowner can more easily manage the risk that is left.

Surprisingly, few real estate agents have this "risk" discussion with their clients. Home buyers NEED this primer on risk and risk management! In the absence of this discussion and education, the buyer ends up without the realization that the risk is all theirs unless they take steps—that is, bear the expense—to utilize risk reduction tools.

It's important to say again that buyers cannot transfer or eliminate ALL risk – that would likely cost more than the home they are purchasing! But through the process of exchanging money for pieces of risk, they can reduce their risk to a more manageable level.

When things go wrong, the buyer most often blames the real estate agent if there is no clear place to obtain compensation for the cost of the item gone wrong! Only when home buyers are well educated by agents about risk and risk reduction tools, do few buyers reject the opportunity to purchase those tools.

Inspection Versus Warranty

The choice between having a home inspection and purchasing a home warranty is a question that I frankly do not understand. Each is intended to serve a separate purpose and ideally they work together to protect the home buyer and reduce the risk of home ownership.

Maybe an analogy will make the matter clear. An individual has just had a complete and thorough physical exam. The results of the exam and all associated lab tests are that the individual appears to free of all disease or illness. This person is presently the picture of health.

Would it be prudent or responsible for the doctor then to recommend to the patient, due to their fine physical condition, that it is a waste of money to continue to pay premiums for health as well as life insurance?

Of course not! None among us would consider the doctor even sane, let alone responsible, if he or she made such a recommendation. But is that not the same situation as someone feeling no need to purchase a home warranty because they just had a home inspection?

And let's view this same scenario from the opposite direction. Would we expect that our life insurance carrier would recommend to us that we forego the expense of regular physical exams, because, after all, we now have life insurance?

INSANITY!

The life insurance companies, in fact, feel so strongly that a physical exam is such an important part of risk reduction that one is often required in order to secure a life insurance policy. Or, at the very least, the exam will affect the insurance rate.

If insurance companies want to have you "inspected" prior to assuming the risk of your passing, it certainly makes sense for the home buyer to have the home inspected prior to purchase. Doesn't it, then, also make similar sense to warrant unforeseen failure with the home warranty?

FSBOs

I'll digress for a moment to talk about FSBO's. To clarify, these are homes "For Sale By Owner" without the use of a real estate agent are affectionately pronounced "fizbo". Not exactly an endearing term, but not altogether derogatory. FSBOs have their own special challenges, especially for home inspectors.

To begin with, it is infrequent that the sellers have ever sold a home before, let alone sold one on their own. And many buyers of the FSBO home are first-time buyers. This sets up the first problem, the blind leading the blind. Remember the previous discussion on risk? There is no one to tell the seller or the buyer about risk reduction tools and why they are important!

Next up is the issue of who stands to gain all the alleged savings of not having to pay the real estate commission. The seller has elected to be a FSBO to save the real estate commission; the buyer often searches out a FSBO in hopes of paying a lower price for the home since there is no real estate commission. Both parties cannot have the same pile of savings! The relationship begins unknowingly in conflict or at least in competition.

Lastly is the problem of emotion ahead of reason. Agents are enough detached from the emotion to provide a clear head to resolve all issues. The seller and buyer have competing needs and interests. That direct competition all too often ends badly.

So it happens that often, the only experienced professional that winds up in the FSBO home with both buyer and seller together at any time during the transaction is the home inspector. If the buyer was wise enough to hire a home inspector! And while many of us inspector types have watched many agents in action, guiding the parties through the details of contract interpretation and negotiation, this is not our responsibility, nor our area of expertise. That being said, in almost every FSBO transaction an inspector winds up in, the inspector ends up in the role of mediator. Every day is an adventure in the life of a home inspector!

Chapter 3
Confessions of a Contract Assassin!

Home buyers are an interesting study. Watching people make their home-buying decisions has brought me to the conclusion that every decision that each one of us makes is based on emotion. You heard me, it's all about the emotion. Before you deny what I am saying to you, let me begin with me.

Painful as the revelation is for me, even I as a Naval Academy graduate, retired Navy pilot, entrepreneur, and home inspector extraordinaire, make decisions based on emotion. It took some significant reflection for me to be able to make this admission, but I am there.

Have you ever had a feeling in your gut about a decision? A hunch? That's emotion. We make decisions that reflect how we feel about the event or expect to feel when the outcome is completed. People, especially those that are highly educated and technically trained, rarely realize and usually never concede that their decisions are based on emotion.

Before discussing the particulars of emotional responses, I will admit that logic does play a role. What ends up happening is, after the near-immediate emotional response and decision, the backfilling of logic begins. Logic is used to make the emotion seem reasonable.

Emotional responses as I see them fall into two broad categories. The first is the desire for pleasure and the second is the avoidance of pain. When we are contemplating a decision, we weigh the balance of the desire for and probability of a pleasurable outcome with the fear of and disdain for pain.

What real estate agents are faced with is responding to issues presented as logic that are actually based on emotion. It takes a tremendous talent to listen to the logic, but hear the emotion. What are people really saying? That is the challenge.

Find and understand the emotional issue and you can keep any deal together. This thought applies no matter if your role is buyer, seller, agent, or inspector. Ultimately, you must seek to understand why people feel as they do in order to fully comprehend what they really mean in what they are saying.

Emotional Hearing Aid

Not long ago, I inspected a home for an electrical engineer, a very bright and successful individual. The home had a beautiful swimming pool in the backyard. Our meticulous engineer had out his digital tape measure and was measuring the distance between each electrical outlet along the rear exterior of the home. He would measure, then ponder, measure more, and then ponder more.

Finally, he approached the real estate agent and me announcing that there was an unsafe condition relating to the unequal distance between the electrical outlets.

He then spouted large quantities of electrical engineer babble and finished with, "I'd be shocked if this were not a code violation". I wanted to respond with, "No, sir, the code is intended to prevent you from being shocked," but decided that "Hmmmm" was a better response.

After much debate and some real listening, I found that the man's issue had nothing to do with electrical engineering or the National Electric Code. In his mind, he had the perfect place for his lounge chair, but there was not an outlet adjacent to that location for him to plug his radio into! He was laying logic, however flawed, on us in order to justify his demand that a new outlet be added.

Listen to the logic, hear the emotion! In my experience, there are four primary emotions that culminate in a home buying decision: fear, anger, sadness, and happiness.

You're Scaring Me!

It must have been told to me a thousand times by real estate agents, "It's not what you say, but how you say it!" And some agents with a little less tact have expanded that concern with, "If you scare my buyer and kill my deal, I will never use your company again!" So now not only is the buyer scared—I am, too!

Sometimes there are issues discovered during the home inspection that are unexpected, confusing, or expensive. An example is a rust-damaged heat exchanger in a gas furnace. The furnace is still making plenty of heat, so it is unexpectedly reported as problematic. This leads to confusion as to why the unit has been declared an issue. The unit is technically broken because the rust holes allow the toxic gases flowing through the unit to mix with the heated air discharged into the room. It is further confusing that it still works! This situation requires immediate replacement with a cost that may well exceed $5,000! And by the way, this problem could kill you while you sleep!

Now that could easily scare someone.

Learning how to make the technical determination that a problem like this exists in a furnace is really rather simple. Developing the ability to understand the emotional aspect is what separates the home inspector technician from the home inspection professional. Doctors do this every day; we call it "bedside manner".

Doctors spend years in school just to earn the right to begin to practice medicine. Then with practice, they learn the fine art of bedside manner. This is what heals us. It took the doctor all these years to understand our body and our particular problem, yet they have only minutes to explain our situation to us and do it in a manner we will understand, all without scaring us to death.

It is my belief that pediatricians would make great home inspectors; their livelihood is much like my own. They deal daily with patients who are completely unfamiliar with what is going on around them, and at the same time the doctor needs to communicate with the   parent. Seems like buyers and agents to me! You know, as I think this through, maybe I should change this thought to—veterinarians would make the best home inspectors. Not only can veterinarians make a diagnosis without dialog with their patients, but also without being bitten!

Those agents that have told me, "It's not what you say, but how you say it" are correct. Home inspectors need a kind of "bedside manner" professionalism in order to best serve their client.

You Made Me Mad!

"This place is a dump! What would make you want to live here anyway?"

Sometimes the reasons why buyers choose to make an offer on a home are a mystery to everyone around the transaction. If the home inspector makes a comment to the buyer that reflects the inspector's dislike for the property without a clear understanding of what beauty the buyer beholds in the property, that sentiment makes buyers mad! Mad is not an emotion that is compatible with positive buying experiences.

As it turns out, the dump in question was a 90-year-old home in great need of renovation. It was clear and obvious that this project would be long, slow, and expensive. What was unknown to the home inspector was that the buyer's great-grandfather had built the home, and both his grandfather and father were born in the home! The buyer had wanted to own, renovate, and raise a family in this home nearly all his life.

The buying decision having been made, the home inspector's role should not have been a commentary on the "dump" status of the home, but rather to expertly and objectively describe the condition of the property so the best renovation plan could be developed for this dream.

Home inspectors must draw the dream from people to understand how best to get technical information delivered into the emotional mind of the buyer to make them understand, not get mad.

You've Made Me Sad

Sometimes a situation arises during the home inspection in which it becomes clear that the problems in a home are of such significance and expense that it is just plain impossible for this particular buyer to buy this particular home. This is always sad.

By the time the home inspection begins, the buyer is really beginning to have an emotional attachment to this home. They have searched for it, studied the neighborhood and the schools, tracked the mileage to work, and spent nights dreaming about this home. They've already made upgrades and renovations in the home, in their minds. They chose this home with both emotion and logic. Now, their heart is in this home.

Come to find out, the dream home needs a new roof, a new kitchen, and has some past termite damage that was never properly repaired. The ticket to correct exceeds $25,000. This is on top of the $10,000 that the buyer had budgeted for a complete cosmetic makeover. The buyer sees no way to manage all of these repairs.

The realization comes that this will not be their dream home, and the buyer is sad.

How we deal with home buyers in this sad situation says quite a bit about who we are, not just as home inspectors, but also as people. This sad time can be made a thankful time when the inspector can help the buyer see that we did not just destroy a dream, but rather prevented a nightmare. Had this home become their home without the newfound knowledge, they would have become mired in a mountain of problems, each jumping out as the other was corrected, and stealing cash and sleep until the home was lost.

You Make Me Glad!

From the initial greeting to the handshake of goodbye, home buyers need to feel glad all along the way that they are having this exciting experience of home inspecting. Glad they chose this home; glad to learn about the home's history and care, even glad to learn of its flaws and foibles.

Buyers feel glad about the experience when the home inspector and agent are working together to support the buyer in the buying decision. Support does not mean disinterested pushiness and flamboyant sales pitches. Support means that all parties in the transaction have come together to fully inform and educate the buyer. Remember, the buyer already loves the home, or the inspection would not be taking place. Now they need final confirmation that the home will live as it looks.

The glad feeing comes when the home buyer looks at the real estate agent and says, "Good deal, flaws and all".

That home buyer will be happy for a long, long time. Not only will they be happy with the home, but also with the home inspector and agent, as well as with the entire team of professionals who participated in making them glad they choose us all!

Burn, Baby, Burn!

Luxury homes are lots of fun to inspect. Sure, the pay is better too, but mostly it's just fun to see how the other half lives! I also get to meet those people who have reached such a level of financial success that they are buying a home that seems like it could have been a boarding school!

One of the fun aspects of inspecting large and expensive homes is seeing furnishings and interior design work at the highest level. Unfortunately, that high level does not always translate to "attractive"! Good-sized decorating budgets do not always mean good taste. One such mansion sticks always in my mind.

Among the oldest and most prestigious sections of Jacksonville is Ortega. Situated along a wide expanse of the St. Johns River with a fabulous view of the downtown skyline is Ortega Boulevard. In our fair town, that address spells success.

It is always a thrill to inspect on Ortega Boulevard. The homes were built during the 1920s and 30s by the business and political leaders of the time. In a state not known for architecture, homes on Ortega Boulevard can be compared proudly with any in America. But that does not mean that some folks don't commit creative crimes in the decorating department!

The listing agent was thrilled to have this home as the cornerstone of an enviable listing portfolio. One point, though, kept coming up in comments made by would-be buyers after being shown the beautiful home. The plum-painted walls on nearly the entire first floor made the interior look like the set from the old *Rowan and Martin's Laugh-In* television show! This simply had to be corrected to attract a buyer to the home.

Upon arrival at the home, I parked behind the painter's truck. When I went into the home, a team of painters was busy working to cover "plum" with "eggshell". Their best guess was that three coats would do it; I was betting on five!

As is always the protocol, all the lights, appliances, and heating were turned on. My company calls this our "Super Bowl" check. Seems that the greatest stresses a home undergoes are during the Super Bowl. There are usually dozens of people around, all of whom are using multiple televisions, cooking, washing, showering, and consuming every possible stitch of electricity. And all of this is going on simultaneously! If the systems continue to work during the Super Bowl, they will work fine during routine family use, or so the theory goes.

So, while I was zipping about the house checking here and checking there, one of the painters called out that he smelled smoke!

If the home catches on fire during the Super Bowl that is most certainly a penalty.

Upon my arrival at the electrical panel, I smelled heat and burning wire. I then ran to the exterior to disconnect power at the switch adjacent to the meter, which was on fire! I told the real estate agent to call the fire department while I secured power to the home. Things were going to be fine.

To my surprise and confusion, the agent became upset with me for securing power to the home. When I asked her why she was upset that I had secured power to the burning electrical panel, she exclaimed, "Wally, if you turn off the power, the painters won't be finished today!"

I reminded her that if the home continued to burn, it wouldn't need paint!

The old adage "When you're surrounded by alligators, sometimes it's hard to remember that you came here to drain the swamp" must have been coined by a guy who was working for a real estate agent in Florida.

Chapter 4
What Qualifies a Home Inspector You Can Trust?

Deal Killers, Contract Assassins, Home Inspectors. Call them what you will, the most important thing is knowing whom to call. But how do you know who to call, and how do you judge their expertise?

Home inspectors are quite simply the objective voice of the home. The mantra of home inspectors should be, "If the home could speak, what would it say?" It is critical that the inspector is able to speak in a manner that makes understanding simple for the home buyer, yet has the depth of technical language to detail necessary repairs using terminology common to the trades.

Choosing the right home inspector is in many ways more difficult than choosing the home. A clear and critical approach to selecting an inspector is essential to being happy over time with the home selected.

You've Got a Friend in Construction

It seems that everyone knows someone who "works in construction", and from that relationship comes the common desire by some buyers to save the professional inspection fee by having the friend or family member perform their home inspection.

At first blush, this seems like a perfect solution. The friend or family member is a known and trusted person. There is no doubt in the mind of the buyer that the loyalty and intentions of this person are above reproach. And then, of course, there is the issue of saving the inspection fee.

The positive attributes of the friend are important. Ideally, all but the expense issue would be traits found in any professional home inspector. The difficulty arises in three principal areas: objectivity, creditability, and inspection-specific knowledge.

Let's look first at the issue of inspection-specific knowledge. While it may be that the friend is without peer in his particular area of construction, it is rare that he is able to view a home in its entirely—that is, as an interaction of dozens of complex and interrelated systems. The most knowledgeable of heating and air-conditioning contractors may know next to nothing about roofing.

Even more common, however, than the lack of a broad base of knowledge, is the lack of any knowledge that is useful during a home inspection.

On more than one occasion when the "friend in construction" has been asked specifically about construction experience or knowledge, it turns out that this actual experience was something other than optimal. This "experience" usually amounts to something along the lines of loading trucks at the hardware store to earn beer money during spring break back in '74! Even with the best of intentions, this is hardly the knowledge needed to guide a friend or family member through what is most likely the largest financial decision of their life.

The Objectivity of My Desire

By their very nature, friends and family members are not objective. They have great compassion for the buyer and likewise great fear that some harm, be that physical or financial, may come to that buyer. Making matters all the worse is the fear in the back of the head of the "friend in construction" that their experience is not truly enough to render the opinions being sought.

This takes the situation down the path to an even less desirable situation. We have a nervous or anxious buyer being given advice by a now nervous and anxious person who is operating well outside their area of expertise. However, they are now reluctant to concede that they are lost and scared. This is not good for anyone in the transaction—buyer, seller, or agent!

Trust and Credibility

Moving on, we come to the issue of credibility. I've observed thousands of transactions, and it seems to me that sellers are a distrusting lot. Or rather, they certainly are when it comes to issues of imperfections in their homes.

What happens if, by some stoke of good fortune, the "friend in construction" actually performs the home inspection in a superior manner, and actually discovers all of the homes flaws in a clear and concise way? It is still probable that the seller will doubt the results are fair and objective due to the relationship between buyer and "inspector".

This inherent distrust most always results in a professional inspector being called in to confirm or deny the observations of the "friend". Who pays the bill for this additional involvement and the issue of what to do with conflicting observations only adds another layer of pain and confusion to a transaction that is already hemorrhaging to death.

Keep life simple. Hire professional inspectors. And if there is a personal connection, be sure to disclose that up front to all concerned. Most people will not object to the disclosure, but let the discovery be made after the fact and the trust, as well as the transaction, may be gone forever.

Inspector or Appraiser?

The respective roles of the appraiser and home inspector are often confused. This confusion has caused many people to falsely believe that the home appraiser was also inspecting the condition of the home. While in a broad sense the appraiser will factor in an obvious deficiency in the condition of the home, it is a factor only in that it affects value.

The confusion between the two activities has brought enough problems to the home-buying process that HUD has developed a mandatory form for FHA loans to ensure that the delineation of responsibilities is clear. The FHA outlines the following:

The responsibilities of the appraiser are:

- To estimate the market value of the house.

- To make sure that the house meets FHA minimum property standards.

- To make sure that the house is marketable.

The responsibilities of the home inspector are:

- To evaluate the physical condition of the structure and systems.

- To identify items in need of repair or replacement.

- To estimate the remaining useful life of the major systems, equipment, structure, and finishes.

The Specialist Assassin

There are some who would say the best inspection is an inspection in which all the trades are represented by a tradesperson from each specialty bringing individual and specific expertise to each system, then reporting separately to the home buyer. This argument supposes that no one knows plumbing better than a plumber, roofs better than a roofer, or electric better than an electrician, etc.

While it is true that the home inspector should utilize specialized equipment such as moisture meters, borescopes, and infrared cameras, I will support the idea that no one knows each trade better than a person specifically from that trade. But, such an approach to home inspecting has several glaring flaws.

Flaw #1. To inspect the entire home using individual trades people would require more than a dozen people. Roofer, plumber, electrician, framer, mason, heating expert, insulation expert, painter, landscaper, pool expert, chimney sweep, appliance expert, tile layer—and we still have windows, doors, and more. For scheduling and crowd control alone, this is a bad idea.

Flaw #2. It would be difficult to find a dozen or more trades people to do this inspection without the appearance of intent to solicit repair work. There is no ethics position that precludes each tradesperson from soliciting work in their chosen trade. That is what people do; they work in their trade.

This looking for work mentality puts the objectivity of the inspection process in jeopardy. While it may be appropriate for the tradesperson to make suggestions for improvement or upgrade to a homeowner, this approach is not best-suited to the buying process, when the goal of the inspection process is principally to determine if existing systems are functioning as intended, and perhaps answer component life expectancy questions.

Flaw #3. The biggest problem, however, with bringing in a dozen trades people to inspect a home is one that cannot be overlooked. In this scenario, no one is charged with the responsibility of putting all the information together, sorting how each item interacts with the others, documenting the concerns in a coherent fashion, and most importantly of all, explaining what it all means to the home buyer in the context of the purchase and sale agreement.

If real estate agents have ever found it a challenge to deal with the issues discovered during a home inspection by a single home inspector, you have GOT to believe that sorting the detail, or lack thereof, from a dozen different trades people is a challenge that might just be insurmountable!

Talk about a state of confusion!

Let's leave home inspecting to the professionally trained home inspector and leave the installation and repair of specific systems to the people who install and repair!

When to Call the Cardiologist

In most instances, the professional home inspector should be able to complete the home inspection without the need to call in specialty expertise. It is the job of the inspector to possess sufficient familiarity with the homes and components typically found in his or her territory to be able to determine what is being inspected and if it is functioning as intended. But, there are times when specific special expertise is warranted.

At all times, it is expected that specialty expertise will be called in to affect repairs. However, it should also be anticipated that the specific expertise of the tradesperson will, from time to time, result in the defect being found different than the home inspector originally described.

The home inspector may have correctly identified a system as not working correctly, but incorrectly identified the specific cause or sub-component that was deficient. The more precise assessment by the tradesperson stems from their greater level of specific expertise. In addition, experts may discover additional defects during repair by their routine use of specialty diagnostic equipment common to a specific trade. This level of knowledge is not routinely available or expected from the home inspector.

This situation is analogous to that of the family doctor who detects some irregularity while listening to someone's heart. The general practitioner may offer some thoughts on potential specifics of the problem. After referral to a cardiologist for specific diagnosis and treatment, it may well be that the initial thoughts of the family doctor were not specifically correct, but there was indeed the need for further treatment. This outcome is still good for the patient!

A similar eye should be used to judge the home inspector when they are perfectly correct that something is wrong and in need of attention, but the detail is imperfect. This situation speaks well to the need to do the due diligence of repair, or at least estimate of repair prior to closing the sale.

Unique Systems

There are some situations when an especially unique system requires specialty expertise just to tell if the system is working. Solar systems would be an example. Another would be a sophisticated electronic control system that needs special diagnostic skills and equipment (think "smart house").

It should never be the case that with every system of the home, the home inspector calls for an expert evaluation. If this does happen, the inspector is usually seeking to reduce his or her own liability. Sometimes, there is a simple lack of technical skills to make basic judgments. If this behavior is routine, this is an inspector to be avoided! The inspector is of little use in getting information to the decision makers or in supporting the transaction in a timely manner.

The Assassin's Tools

What else qualifies a home inspector? The tools used! The home inspection profession has come a long way, especially in terms of the equipment we now use. Along with more standard "tools of the trade", experienced and tech savvy inspectors use pole cameras, moisture meters, borescopes, and infrared cameras, as well as computers to generate color, digital, email-able reports.

What is infrared? I'm glad you asked!

Way back when people were living in caves, the cave inspector behaved much like regular home inspectors do to this day. They brought light into the cave to see what they could see. As time went on, the tools to produce light got better and better.

Cave inspectors got light into the cave with a torch; log cabin inspectors got light into the cabin with a lantern; ultimately, yesteryear's home inspectors got light into the home with a flashlight. Interestingly, the light of the torch illuminated the walls about as well as regular inspectors illuminate your walls with a flashlight. They can only see what is visible.

But what if you could see what is INVISIBLE?

Beyond the visible light spectrum is the infrared spectrum. Infrared is invisible to the naked eye. But with state of the art infrared thermal imaging cameras, tech-savvy inspectors can now "see" what is invisible to regular inspectors.

In simplest terms, infrared cameras represent temperature readings as a full color image. It's as though each of the thousand pixels on the camera screen were a thermometer, each individual thermometer displaying a color to represent its temperature reading. The colors of each pixel weave together to display an image. This results in a clear image to distinguish a wet wall from a dry wall, a hot wire from a cold wire, and a damaged duct from an in-tact duct.

Infrared technology makes it simple to comfort a home buyer as well as protect the home seller and any real estate agents. Peace of mind does not come from a stone-age inspector raising questions, and then leaving them unanswered. Peace of mind comes from knowing PRECISELY what the visual symptoms really mean. That level of confidence can only be reached with the use of an infrared camera in the hands of an educated and experienced home inspector. It is little wonder that infrared cameras have been called the most significant advancement in home inspections since the invention of the flashlight!

Another modern advancement in home inspection tool technology is the digital borescope. This is the precise technology that your doctor would use to perform a colonoscopy. A long flexible tube with a lighted on camera on one end sends a color picture to the digital display screen on the other end. This device can be snaked into duct work, behind equipment and into the smallest of spaces and places to revel secrets that would have previously been undiscoverable without destructive entry into the space.

Much like the example of the colonoscopy, most times the tool determines that there is no need for concern. But, without the borescope to examine the area of concern there are questions unanswered and fear of the unknown often remains.

Also among the advancements that have become an expectation of the modern home inspector is Internet access from the home during the home inspection. The information instantly available online is used by the home inspector to confirm upgrade dates with building departments, search property appraiser data bases, and research manufactures websites. This ability to research and verify onsite is invaluable to providing peace of mind to the home buyer while ensuring fair and accurate representation of the sellers property.

Many inspectors will tell you that their inspection is visual, done to a generalist level. I agree – that's true of all home inspections! But now that the technology to be even more thorough and detailed is here, inspectors should embrace it and offer it to their clients. Why? Because clients want and demand it, for peace of mind!

Assassins Will Do Anything

I've always maintained that all home inspectors must be willing to get down and dirty for their clients. During an inspection, inspectors will not only see some very beautiful and awe-inspiring homes, but will find themselves in very unappealing and even frightening places, most notably the attic and crawl space. For me, among a great group of memorable belly crawls, one stands out above, or maybe I should say below, all the others.

One fine day I was called to do an inspection of a lovely two-story home in the historic and trendy Ortega section of Jacksonville. The home was built off-grade and had a larger than typical crawl space. It was at least eighty feet from one end to the other. If dog years are seven times longer than people years, then me crawling on my belly makes a crawl space seven times longer than if a dog were walking the same distance. I had to crawl over 500 dog feet! This is a long way to belly crawl.

Nothing major occurred or was observed on the initial inspection, although there was some wood rot on the sub-floor under the master bathroom. I was a tired puppy when I got out of the crawl.

On the morning of settlement, I got a frantic call from the buyer's agent. The buyer was in a panic about the quality and completeness of the repairs to the bathroom sub-floor. The buyer was refusing to close on the sale unless my trusted eye viewed the repair. Not wanting to disappoint and always enjoying the role of real estate hero, over to Ortega I drove.

From my last visit to the home, I was expecting an easy time of it, aside from the long length of belly crawling. I was wrong! Heavy rains had flooded the crawl space; there was at least six inches of water on the floor of the crawl space! If this was a distance best traveled by a dog, it would have best been done by a Labrador! The pressure was on to perform.

Into the garage I went, alone, got down to my birthday suit, and put on my crawl space suit. Back out to the crawl space entrance, where the buyer and agent were looking at me in disbelief that I was about to go swimming under the home. It was all rather Rambo-like, frogs hopping and croaking all along the way!

Arriving at the repair was anti-climactic. It looked great. I was real thankful for this, as I had no desire to return to re-inspect. The buyer and agent were elated with the news and drove off to the closing. I was left wet and alone. Such is the life of the home inspector.

Chapter 5
How Should a Home Be Judged?

When seeking a reasonable expectation of a home, the first question that needs to be addressed is the standard by which the home should be judged. Expectation mandates that some standard be offered against which we create, base, and manage our expectations.

I Want Perfection

A common, though problematic, standard upon which to form the basis of expectation in homes is the standard of perfection. Certainly there are reasons that people would desire this to be the condition of the home. It's easy to see how this thought gets into the minds of some home buyers.

Most people are considering buying a particular home to be rid of some imperfection in their existing living quarters. It may be as simple as having outgrown the previous home or wanting to be closer to work. Sometimes for the first-time buyer it is simply the idea of home ownership. But for some reason, or more often for a collection of reasons, buyers usually feel that the physical condition of the home should be perfect.

The Problem with Perfection

So, what is wrong with perfection as the standard by which the home inspector should judge the condition of a home? It's quite simple, really—there are no perfect houses! And if we were to attempt to build one that was perfect, no one would agree on what perfect was and the cost would be exorbitant!

I have a saying. Are you ready for this? Brace yourselves . . .

"Houses are like spouses..."

Wait, there's more!

"...There are no perfect choices, but the consequence of poor choice can be miserable".

(Not to mention, expensive!)

As you are recovering from this saying, really think about it. This saying is the ultimate standard by which to judge houses!

"New" Be the Judge

Perfect having been discovered to be an imperfect expectation by which to measure the performance of homes, let's consider the idea of judging every home against a home that was built today. This seems an ideal idea. When speaking to many groups of both consumers and agents, most initially agree this is a standard that is reasonable.

But when considered against specific examples, the idea begins to lose its luster.

Imagine for the moment a charming home built during the 1930s, perhaps a bungalow in the arts and crafts style so admired today. Among other fabulous details, it has glistening hardwood floors, detail moldings on every ceiling, and original brass fixtures lighting every room. This home is, to those who have an eye for such things, gorgeous! But wait, what about those ungrounded electrical outlets and asbestos shingles on the roof? Surely, those are a problem!

Problem, What Problem?

People want to know if they have problems! This is the very reason why we have regular physical exams and why we take our automobiles to the mechanic for inspections at prescribed mileages. We know we do not want problems. But, back to real estate, what is a problem?

Since the dawn of the real estate contract, lawyers and agents have sought to define problems in homes. The thought has always been, if problems are defined, those problems would not become obstacles to the contractual issues in closing the deal when discovered during the home inspection process. Most efforts by lawyers and agents to define problems in homes have attempted to create a list by including or excluding those issues that most commonly disrupt deals in that specific locale.

The problem with this approach to managing problems is that it was developed to expedite the contract. It does not reflect the fears, emotions, and needs of the parties directly involved namely the buyer and seller. That is to say, if we are working with a list of items that the contract says are problems, it is unlikely that every item on this list would be similarly judged as problematic by both the buyer and the seller.

To Define and Prevent

Every list that has ever been made attempting to fully and completely address and define "problems" that could reasonably be expected to be corrected by the seller has FAILED. These lists have failed because, by their very nature, lists seek to include and exclude. They include for consideration only those items on the list and then by default those items not on the list are excluded from consideration. Such is the nature of lists, be they shopping lists, to do lists, or real estate repair request lists in a contract.

Lists, quite simply, always fail us!

So, what's a smart person to do? In my mind, small though active as it is, the answer lies in a simple and succinct definition of what a "problem" is!

A problem is, our legal buddies would tell us, "something not functioning as intended".

I love this definition! It is simple. It is succinct! And darn if it doesn't work in every situation. Let's test it.

Let's revisit the issue of ungrounded electrical outlets. You know the ones—they have only two holes for the plug prong instead of the presently-prescribed three-hole outlets. Are they a problem? Every time I ask this question, most people reply with "yes".

I can understand why most would think that two-hole outlets are a problem. There are usually several good reasons behind that first guess of "yes". The two-hole electrical outlets lack a third hole for the ground wire of most modern appliances. Sure enough, this lack of ground does increase the potential for both electrical shock and electrical damage to equipment. Also, when the ugly question of code is asked, no, the two-hole ungrounded outlets do not meet present requirements of The National Electrical Code (more on code later). Surely, this is a problem!

Now, back to our definition of a problem, "something not functioning as intended". If when the home was built, the electrical system was installed to meet the existing electrical code and the system, in this case specifically the ungrounded electrical outlet, remains in its original configuration and is functioning as intended, do we have a problem?

NO!

No ifs, ands, buts, or what-abouts, if the outlet is functioning as it was intended, then it is not a problem. Should it be correctly disclosed, described, and documented as an ungrounded electrical outlet? Certainly, but to put it in simplest terms, "if it ain't broke, don't fix it!"

Buy Me a 1955 Ford T-Bird

Here's a quick analogy to hammer the point home. In my mind, one of the most beautiful cars ever manufactured was the 1955 Ford Thunderbird. You know the one, it's the car that Robert Urich drove as Dan Tanna on the television detective show *Vegas*. And the same car introduced Suzanne Somers to the world in the motion picture *American Graffiti*. I just love that car! (Editor's note: While Wally maintains that the *American Graffiti* car was a 1955, a Google search revealed that it was actually a 1956. Just wanted to set the record straight.)

But when we get technical about it all, skip the emotion brought on by the mere mention of that car and what have we got? A fifty-year-old Ford that lacks every modern safety and comfort feature! No air bags, no anti-lock brakes, no power steering, and no air-conditioning. By today's standards, that car makes a Geo Metro look like a Maserati!

All that being true, why then do I lust for this car?

Simple...owning this car would make me feel good!

Is this logical? No. Is my dream car technically unsafe? Sure. But, must it be brought up to current "car code" at the time of sale by installing air bags and anti-lock brakes? No.

All of these technical things about the car simply don't matter as they relate to the presently-accepted safety practices of today. If it were in the proper working condition, my 1955 Thunderbird would be "functioning as intended!"

Why then can we not apply the same thought and reason to our view of houses? If the home was built in 1955 with two-hole ungrounded electrical outlets and they are functioning as intended, well then, it just is as it is, and it is fine!

All Problems Are Not Created Equal

Now that the problem of "problems" has been solved simply with the "functioning as intended" definition, we can move on. It often happens that when the home buyer gets comfortable with the "if it ain't broke, don't fix it" approach, the next leap is to assume, or at least desire that all problems discovered with the home during the home inspection will be corrected by the seller. This is a reasonable leap, but not one that typically results in a happy home seller.

In the mind of the seller, nothing should be corrected; in the mind of the buyer, everything should be corrected; and in the mind of the agent who is trying to appease both parties and move to closing, something should be corrected!

If we can agree that all problems are not equal, and also that the typical desires of buyers and sellers regarding repairs are in conflict, perhaps some additional definition is in order. Let's break problems down into two broad and general categories, "major problems," and "minor problems".

Majors and Minors

Let's create a list of major and minor problems. Wait! We already know that lists don't work! There are simply too many systems, and too many perspectives to create a list. So, more definitions are in order.

A major problem we will define as:

Something not functioning as intended that has a cost to remedy of more than $1000 or presents a real and present danger.

Neat and clean, nice and tight.

Now on to the minor problem, which we will define as:

Something not functioning as intended that has a cost to remedy that is less than $1000 or is a deferred maintenance or cosmetic concern.

Buyers most always consider these parameters reasonable and readily accept them. Agents often balk at the inclusion of cosmetic concerns, feeling that they have no place in the inspection or transaction. If what seems right and reasonable to the buyer does not seem so to the agent, Houston, we have a problem! After some consideration, and with a wealth of input from agents, the following addition has come:

Most major problems are the responsibility of the seller, and most minor problems the responsibility of the buyer. The contract will address specifics.

This approach works very well. It works especially well if all parties agree at the time of contact, and certainly if they agree before the home inspection.

All About Peer Pressure

If we embark on a journey to complete my dream of owning my very own 1955 Ford Thunderbird, we might need to look at a dozen of them to make the right buying decision. We would find some that look like they just drove off the showroom floor, and some in such a sad state that many would consider them unsalvageable.

And the price spread! At the high end, some of these 50-year-old beauties are over $50,000, while those that would be life-long renovation projects might be tens of thousands less.

So which 1955 Thunderbird do we choose? Having looked at dozens of similar cars, in every condition and price range, with every possible problem and a full range of renovation situations, we make a value judgment considering price, present condition, and issues outstanding.

What was that? How did we make our decision? We did a peer-to-peer comparison to make the best choice for our budget, taste, and temperament. That process worked well!

Back to the example of the home with ungrounded electrical outlets. All the homes built in 1955 have two-hole ungrounded outlets; that is the expectation of that peer group. No sense looking for one built to a standard that is in effect 50 years later, because there aren't any!

If the attraction is to a peer group that has a characteristic deemed unacceptable, choose a different peer group. Stop looking for a 1955 Thunderbird with air bags! There are none! A feature failing to function is a problem; the absence of the feature is NOT a problem.

The same is true of the home built in 1955. Enjoy its charms, cherish its history, but do not see problems with features that are actually functioning as intended.

When considering which home to make an offer on, we should always go through this process of a peer-to-peer comparison. It just so happens that peer-to-peer comparisons are perfect for car selection, home selection, and home inspection!

Get Perspective!

By now, we are past the point of expecting perfection. We're also comfortable with a peer-to-peer comparison being the key to a happy buying decision.

But what of those pesky imperfections? How do we best view and present each and every imperfection to ensure a full and complete disclosure concerning the home, while at the same time keep the romance in the buying decision?

The home and the home inspection must be continually viewed in the greater context of why the buyer originally chose to make an offer on the home to begin with. What were the charms and features that made it attractive? What personal and professional activities are more convenient at this location? How will life be better living here? Too often in the turmoil of the transaction, home buyers forget their original desires and then question why they are buying the home.

When a home buyer seems to be stressing to the extreme over minor issues or imperfections, it is most always due to a loss of perspective. When the oven that has a broken three-dollar knob or the running toilet that needs a ten-dollar flushing mechanism seems destined to doom the deal, take a break! Perspective is needed and needed fast.

When all of the professionals involved in the transaction share in the joys and dreams of the buyer for their chosen home, it really helps the buyer keep a focused perspective. Sure, the process can be a bit spooky. But, it is important that the buyer **not** get bogged down in the process.

Agents, participate in helping the buyer maintain perspective. Enjoy the dreams and delights that are inherent in every residential real estate deal.

Imperfect Perspectives

As a man who spends his life around real estate agents, I routinely hear their thoughts, concerns, and beliefs. Many of these agents express a fear that if a home buyer is fully informed about the imperfections of a home it will kill the deal. While it is true that a long list of problems can frighten some people, I've seen deals made in spite of what seem to be huge issues. Sometimes the reason that someone selects a home is precisely because of a particular imperfection.

Several years ago, I did a home inspection for a young couple buying their first home. The dream of the wife was to live in a section of town called Mandarin. The husband was a roofer, a fine fellow who wanted nothing but to give his wife her dream of living in Mandarin. However, this was a neighborhood slightly beyond their budget.

After showing the young couple many homes in Mandarin to no avail, their agent explained that there were no homes in their area of choice that fit their budget. Home after beautiful home, the prices were just too high.

Meanwhile, also in Mandarin, there was a home seller who had given up hope of ever selling his home. It had been on the market with an agent for six months, but no sale. The poor home needed a new roof and the seller's financial situation precluded that issue from being worked into the deal.

It seemed that every agent in town knew of the bad roof, and would always drive right by the tainted house. Frustrated, the seller allowed the listing agreement to expire.

After months and months of searching, our roofer family was driving around without their agent one Saturday, dreaming of a home in Mandarin. Frustrated and just about to give up on their dream of owning a home in Mandarin, they happened to drive past the home with the bad roof, and saw our seller pounding his "For Sale By Owner" sign into the front yard. They had been in the area several times looking at other homes with their agent, and simply assumed this house was out of their budget, just like all the rest. However, the FSBO sign made them stop. Bit-a-bang, bit-a-boom—home under contract on the spot!

What happened?!

The home needed a roof and was priced accordingly. But agent after agent had made a value judgment on the home, killing deals before they had a chance to breathe. This home was precisely what the young couple needed!

For just a few hundred dollars in materials and the help of some roofer buddies, the home got a new roof. The deal closed, dreams came true, and everyone lived happily ever after. Everyone, that is, except the agents who were no longer involved!

The Buyers' Every Desire!

It has always amazed me the things you can get when you ask! While contract and experience might tell us that a particular request has no chance of being granted, we only have one certainty—if we do not ask, we will get nothing.

I have known buyers to get everything from new carpet to tropical fish included in the deal, simply by asking. These requests have been most successful when they were part of the original offer. Sometimes, the request has resulted in a higher sales price. This never seems to bother the agents. And on other occasions, especially with those requests dealing with personal property, that portion of the deal was done outside the bounds of the contract. The important point is to include every desire in the original offer. That is why it is called an offer.

As an example, many contracts have attempted to address the issue of "fogged" windows. This "fogging" occurs when the seal is disrupted between the glass of double pane windows. Everyone agrees that this discoloration is unsightly, but few agree on whether it is a "cosmetic" condition. If deemed cosmetic, it would be reasonably expected that the buyer correct the problem. If deemed a more substantial issue, then the seller would be reasonably expected to stipulate a remedy within the repair or inspection section of the contract.

Some contracts read in favor of this situation being cosmetic, while others read in favor of it being a substantial issue. Regardless of how it reads, when the widow glass is fogged, one party likes the contract; the other feels they are being unfairly treated. This situation is best addressed in the original offer rather than waiting for the home inspection.

During the negotiation process, there tends to be a desire to reduce the number of items to be repaired. If items that were identifiable by the home buyer before the home inspection are not included in the original offer, there may not be another opportunity to address those items. Always include in the original offer any known, disclosed, or observed items that need repair. It always makes the deal simpler.

Please, always include the buyers' every desire in the original offer. You can't get what you don't ask for, and sometimes you can't get what you don't ask for *early*.

Chapter 6
Why Do Assassins Have Contracts?

Real estate transactions live or die on documentation. The purchase and sale agreement is only the beginning of the paper trail to home ownership. It's also the beginning of the path to agents receiving commission. It has been said that a verbal agreement is not worth the paper that it is printed on. I agree with that. The true purpose of a properly-written contractual document is to define expectation, to reduce the likelihood for disappointment, and to provide a resolution method should conflict arise.

For the agent, the inspection contract describes and binds the relationship between buyer and inspector. As an agent with a contractual relationship with the buyer and possibly also with the seller, you would not want the inspector in the transaction without a written contract, lest any potential conflicts fall to you.

By the time the home buyers and inspector meet, the buyers are getting pretty good at reviewing documents and signing their names. Rarely has a person taken issue with an element in my company's inspection agreement. But one such occasion stands out.

The Florida Lottery has made some instant millionaires; in fact, some instant mega millionaires. One of these fortunate fellows was also to become my client.

Ever notice that sometimes the wealthy get wealthier and the lucky get luckier? This particular lucky and wealthy fellow had retired in his forties, having been a very successful lawyer who also invested very well. It had become his habit in retirement to walk to the neighborhood convenience store each morning for a cup of coffee, the newspaper, and a lottery ticket. Just a fun morning event, but this gentleman ends up with a winning ticket worth tens of millions of dollars!

So what issue could a mega-millionaire retired attorney have with my inspection agreement? Our agreement has a "loser pays legal fees" statement. My mega-millionaire-lawyer client told me he had made some change to every contract he had ever signed, and my contract would not be the first to miss his scrutiny. So what did he try to change? He wanted to cross out my right to collect legal fees! Lawyers, gotta love 'em!

Aspects of an Assassins Agreement

Home inspections have become so much a part of the home-buying process that most of what goes on seems routine. But it is important that the routine be consistent and predictable. The inspection contract or agreement provides that framework for consistency.

Most inspection agreements are more in-depth than will be discussed here, but there are four key items to look at that are shared by all good inspection agreements. Those are:

1. Name the parties involved in the contract, and define the responsibilities of the buyer and the   inspector to each other.

2. Define the scope of the inspection, and outline any state licensing compliance.

3. Outline remedies to resolve differences should they occur.

4. Define any exclusions to the inspection service, or items not inspected.

1. Naming the Assassin's Target

The first thing the inspection agreement does is to name the parties to the inspection contract. More often than not, the parties are the home buyer and the home inspector. Never confuse who is paying for a service and who the client for that service may be. The client's name goes onto the contract regardless of who is paying.

Some agents offer to pay for the buyer's inspection as a marketing expense. This is great! But, this does not make the agent the client. The responsibilities of the buyer to the inspector, and vice versa, do not change.

2. The Assassin's Scope

The scope of the inspection describes what the home inspector will inspect and the basic methods of inspection. It should also outline any state licensing compliance issues. This is a critical area to understand.

The home inspection is typically limited to a visual examination to a generalist standard. It is not intended to be or represented as an engineering study or technically-exhaustive evaluation. Sophisticated equipment or techniques may or may not be employed – although, as mentioned earlier, I maintain that the inspector you choose should be utilizing, at the very least, a moisture meter, borescope, and infrared camera along with the other more standard "tools of the trade".

3. Conflict Resolution

It is important that the agreement contain a provision for the resolution of conflict between the parties involved. Conflict is never fun. It is best avoided by establishing at the outset how to solve any problems that might arise. This process simply prevents even more problems.

When a client turned homeowner becomes unhappy with something they believe to be the fault of the home inspector, it is best that they first review the original report to see if the item causing the displeasure was a reported item and then to review the resolution section of the inspection agreement.

We once had an unfortunate situation with a past client. After having removed the wallpaper in a bathroom, the owner noticed a previously-patched area of drywall that was poorly done. The owner then removed that small section of drywall with the intent to replace it properly.

Now with this small section of wall opened, he noticed that a rodent had at one time made the area under the bathtub a cozy home. This really distressed Mrs. Homeowner, who encouraged Mr. Homeowner to remedy the situation fast!

Ideally, what should have happened at this point was a call be placed to the home inspector to seek advice and counsel. We do this every day. Past clients have new problems and we make every effort to get them pointed in the right direction. In this particular case, the original home inspection had documented a pest problem in the attic. Had the home buyers acted on this information, the solution to that rodent sighting in the attic would have probably solved this second sighting in the bathroom.

But that didn't happen.

For a reason I will never know, Mr. Homeowner went in pursuit of the rodent. The walls of the bathroom were removed, as was the bathtub! Still no rodent, just more nesting material. At this point we have, I am sure, a rather tense situation at home! So, what does Mr. Homeowner do? He called my office, his home inspection company, requesting money to restore the bathroom. And he would rather we put in a shower instead of a tub!

Anyway, the moral of the story is read your contract, and if you have a problem, any problem, call anytime.

That is, any time BEFORE you destroy your bathroom!

4. The Assassin Missed!

There are, for sure, certain spaces and places that the home inspector will be unable to inspect. These specific locations should be exempted in the inspection contract and documented as un-inspected in the written report.

The three most common reasons for exempting a system or component from inspection are:

- Areas or actions deemed dangerous

- Action, which might damage the home

- Seasonal limitations

Danger to the Assassin

To kill the inspector in the process of the inspection will only slow the transaction. Plus it really makes the buyer feel bad.

Obviously, it is a limitation of the inspection process when some item, if properly or completely inspected, poses a physical danger to the inspector. A common example of an inappropriate risk posed to an inspector would be a wet roof with an extremely steep pitch.

Good inspectors will walk on most roofs. But if it is slicker than snake snot, it's just too dangerous! When a roof is too dangerous to walk on, the inspector may view it from the ground, often with binoculars. The inspector may also choose to view the roof from the top of a ladder placed at locations around the home.

An inspection of the roof from the ground is clearly not as good as if the roof were walked in its entirety. There are often portions of the roof that are not visible due to obstructions posed by chimneys or dormers. These "invisible" areas are at a high risk of problem. To help reduce risk, it may be possible to access these areas by looking out windows or via attic crawl areas, but it is still a less certain process. Physically walking the roof is always the best scenario.

However, in the example of the wet roof with a steep pitch, it would not be prudent for the inspector to walk the roof. Best to see all that can be seen, and document the situation.

Damage to the Target

Buyers want and deserve the best inspection that the inspector is able to deliver. Good inspectors want to deliver the finest information possible to the home buyer. Sellers, however, are not too keen on their home being damaged in the process.

There are times when an item will "fail under test". This happens most often when a system seldom if ever used by the seller is operated in all its many and normal modes and breaks in the process. The inspector did not break it. It just broke.

Then again, there are times when the inspector does break something. What happens if the inspector's ladder falls through the dining room window? The inspector should expect to compensate the seller for the window!

Yes, there is a difference between a door that has not been used in years falling off of its rusty hinge and the inspector putting his foot through the ceiling. In the case of the door, it "failed under test," and in the case of the ceiling, the inspector broke it. The seller should not expect compensation to come for damage to the door.

Another example of an exempted item might be an older wood shingle roof. It might not be leaking a drop, but let a big-footed home inspector walk all over it and something bad is bound to happen. These wood shingles, especially as they age, are very susceptible to cracking and breaking. This is a risk to the roof that is best not taken!

No need to damage something just to demonstrate its vulnerabilities. Good inspectors always look out for these situations, and will never knowingly or intentionally damage anything during a home inspection.

There are times when things do end up broken; my own damaging actions seem to happen most often in the kitchen, but usually with help.

My usual kitchen inspection activity is to turn on everything simultaneously. I reason that is how real cooks cook! On one occasion, not having peeked into the dishwasher before turning it on, I thoroughly washed, then dried, a loaf of bread! This made quite a mess and did take some time to clean out. I offered to pay for the bread, but the seller got such joy at watching me clean the mush out of the dishwasher that she passed on the payment offer.

On another kitchen inspection, I managed to broil several pieces of Tupperware into a gooey mess of molten muck!

One last kitchen fiasco—while testing a microwave oven, I placed a wet bandana that was sitting on the sink faucet into the microwave, selected "popcorn" mode and hit start.

Unbeknownst to me, there was a metal clip on the bandana. The microwave started to arc and spark just as the bandana burst into flames! I suppose if I spent more time in the kitchen at home, I would do less damage during inspections.

Seasonal Exclusions

A third common reason to exclude the complete inspection of a particular item is seasonal limitations. I'll take some license at this point and use another roof example—snow. Why is this an inspection limitation?

I must digress at this point in the name of full disclosure. My personal inspection experience has been in over 5,000 houses and our company is nearing 35,000 as I write. The truth is, they have all been in Florida! The snow limitation exclusion is from my inspector buddy George Cline in Rochester, New York. He tells me they have snow on the roofs from Labor Day until Memorial Day!

Snow is a seasonal limitation to George principally because it limits his ability to observe. The snow not only prevents George from climbing safely onto the roof, but also obscures observation from the ground. In addition, the gutters are covered and often the plumbing vents are as well. Meanwhile, down on the ground, the air-conditioner is covered in snow. Even the slope of the ground is often masked by the wind-driven drifts. The inspector must make a best guess on many of these limitations, usually because his eyeballs are frozen. Maybe people living in the Tundra should only buy homes in summer?

Since I've fully disclosed my lack of real-live snow experience, I will share a seasonal limitation from my own area. In Florida, a very common seasonal limitation is associated with air-conditioning systems. When the temperature drops below 60 degrees, we are unable to fully operate the air-conditioning system or the cooling function of heat pump systems. Does this mean those systems are un-inspected? No. It only means that they were not fully OPERATED as part of the inspection!

Let me explain. There is an important distinction between not inspected and not operated. Staying with the air-conditioning example, the inspection of the age, make, model, physical condition, and present maintenance status in and around the system are all accomplished with the system off. The only part of the inspection not completed is the functional check.

Yes, it is a better inspection when the functional check is completed, but it is rare that the functional check reveals an outcome other than would have been expected from the other parts of the system inspection. The functional check is what sticks in the mind of the home buyer, so it is critical to explain the exemption of the functional check as well as document it in the written report.

A Sad Use of an Exemption

Not long ago, I was called in to consult on behalf of a young family who had made their first home purchase the previous year. Kara, the home buyer, and her husband, had purchased a 35-year-old home made of block with a lovely brick front.

It was a charming first home. They hoped to live there long and happy. Shortly after moving in happy, however, continuing to be happy with their choice of home began to escape them.

Kara's story could be a book in itself. In fact, it was later filmed for an episode of *House Detective* on Home and Garden Television (HGTV).

Kara was having problems with mold and moisture in her home. She had a home inspection prior to the purchase of the home, but nothing was brought to her attention that would have given her cause for concern. The house, though, after having been lived in for a while, always seemed to be damp and musty. She even had mold growing on her slippers!

When I am called in to give a second opinion, I will oftentimes not view the report of the previous inspector until after I have made my initial observations and assessments. This, I believe, prevents my own judgment from being clouded by placing preconceived ideas in my mind.

So, progressing through my inspection of her home, I discovered that she had several significant issues in both her attic and in the crawl space below. I was amazed to find that both areas were soaking wet and covered with mold and fungus. This mold and fungus was consuming the wood structure of the roof and was growing in the ductwork. This damage was significant and immediately obvious upon entering the crawl space.

The attic, however, could not be crawled easily; but most areas were visible through an access hatch and by the removal of suspended ceiling tiles. I was completely stunned that this readily apparent moisture and damage had escaped the original inspector upon whom Kara had relied.

When I reviewed the report that Kara had used to base her buying decision, how she had gotten into this situation became clear. There was no mention of any of the problematic issues!

Kara was appalled that something so obvious had been missed! But as we read on, it became clear that the inspector did not miss anything. He merely exempted those areas from the report! He never went into the crawl space nor removed the ceiling tiles to view the attic.

I have always maintained that all the most important discoveries in home inspection are made by going places that are unpleasant to go or where people seldom are.

On the roof, in the attic, and under the house are not fun places to climb or crawl, but that is where inspectors must go to best protect the client. There are times when those locations cannot be completely inspected due to physical risk to the inspector, risk to equipment, or seasonal limitations. But to use an inspection exemption as a way to avoid going into or onto an unpleasant location is completely unacceptable. Watch out for this. Do not accept this practice.

Ample Assassins

A comical side note to this discussion is the physical condition of some inspectors. Someone lacking the physical skills to "climb the climb" or "crawl the crawl" should simply not be a home inspector. They are a danger to themselves and bring unneeded risk to the home buyer. Always ask about an inspector's ability to do the work necessary to complete the inspection.

I mentioned earlier that Kara's home was later the subject of an episode of *House Detective*. That being said, Kara's first home inspector documented that the opening to the crawl space was too small to access. I must tell you that at one point during the television shoot, however, we had nearly 20 people in that same crawl space at the same time!

Imagine homeowners, repair people, inspectors, and a full television crew on their bellies scotching around under this home! The largest of the men had to be nearly 300 pounds. Limited access, my foot!

Chapter 7
What If You Had a Party and Nobody Came?

The purpose of the home inspection is to provide an objective overview of the home under consideration by the buyer. At the conclusion of every inspection there is a written report generated. This documentation is vital to the purchase decision and has a significant standing within the purchase and sale contract, especially within the repair sections.

Should Buyers Be Invited?

Ultimately, the written report takes on amazing clarity when the home buyer is present at the inspection. This is especially true when the inspector generates the written report on site and delivers it to the buyer and agents at the conclusion of the inspection.

It is not possible to cover in even the most technically exhaustive written report all the detail needed to get the most benefit from the inspection. Full color photographs are a great addition to the written report, but it is still an incomplete experience without the involvement of the buyer with the inspector.

It is certainly true that the responsibility for the inspection rests solely with the inspector, but the understanding of the inspection is a shared responsibility between the home buyer and home inspector. This responsibility can best be shared one to the other when buyer and inspector are together during the entire inspection.

When the buyer and inspector are together, any unclear points made by the inspector can be immediately questioned by the buyer. The experienced inspector can then judge the level of understanding, concern, and anxiety of the buyer, not only by the questions asked, but also as importantly by tone and posture. These vital communication exchanges are lost if the buyer is not present and relies only on the written report.

Complaints

Another amazing thing occurs when the buyer and inspector are together for the inspection. Complaints about the inspection after the home buyer become the homeowner drop to near zero! This is a significant plus to buyer, seller, inspector, and agent. When people understand their home—its strengths, weaknesses, beauty, and flaws—they have a perspective on the home and the home inspection processes that is good.

Real estate agents continue to share with me on a near daily basis their concerns about the legal risks of being an agent. No agent wants to be sued. Home inspectors are also not fond of being sued. The best way to not get sued is to have happy clients.

When complaints come into my office, they are taken very seriously. At the risk of giving telemarketers the secret to getting through to me, I will tell you that complaints go right to the top of the heap. They must be handled promptly and professionally.

The desire to reduce complaints to zero has prompted much study of each complaint. An interesting statistic has come from the dissection of complaints. In over 90 percent of the complaint cases, the buyer did not attend the inspection! When the inspector and buyer integrate together in the process of the inspection, things go well.

If some unforeseen event comes the buyer's way after closing, in most cases the buyer recognizes the fault or non-fault of the inspector.

Want to drop that rate to darn near zero? Our data shows us that for our inspection company we will have one complaint for about every 500 inspections. Less would be preferred, but this really is very low. The data also shows us that in only 20 percent of those complained-about inspections did both buyer and agent attend. Doing the math tells me that only 2 percent of our complaints have had both buyer and agent attending together! If my hypothesis holds true, if buyer and agent both attended the inspection, our complaint rate would drop to one complaint in every 2500 home sales! Being that most complaints are easily solved, this rate would be fantastic for buyers, sellers, agents, and us.

Please, whoever you are, whatever your role in the transaction, come to the home inspection!

Buyer Basic Training

The primary responsibility of the home buyer during the home inspection is to observe and to listen. By watching what the inspector does, the home buyer will gain a comfort with the home as well as the inspection process. The inspector has the opportunity to present to and discuss with the home buyer all the many aspects of each component and system in the home.

By observing and listening, the home buyer will gain great comfort with what systems are installed in their home-to-be, the age of those systems, life expectancies of similar systems, general system care, indications of past or present dysfunction, and approximate costs to repair. Most often, the items covered during the inspection can be explained faster, easier, and more clearly simply by pointing to each item, rather than trying to explain the same items later page by page absent the buyer's presence. The goal is to have no issues looming after the inspection.

You Wanna Get High With Me?

Participating in the home inspection is always a good thing. How much to participate is an often debated question. Depending on an individual's role in the transaction—buyer, seller, agent, or other interested party—the intentions, interest, and involvement vary widely.

A sure-fire test to tell how committed someone is to the participation process is to ask who would like to go onto the roof. Many of my home inspector buddies cringe when I speak of home buyers or agents climbing roofs with me. However, with some good judgment and a few precautions, it turns out just fine.

The fun begins when I ask, "Okay, who would like to get high with me?" If anyone looks too enthused, I get a little nervous thinking that they must have misinterpreted my question. But, after a moment, most all recognize that it is time for the roof inspection. No better way to inspect a roof than to climb up and walk around!

Every now and then, a home has a walk-out balcony that lets us hop the rail and stride smartly to the peak. But more often than not, it is up the ladder we go.

The truth of it all is that less than 20 percent of home buyers will venture up the ladder to stroll their roof. And of that group, about half are wearing inappropriate shoes or clothing for the ladder climb. A relatively small number of those who choose to climb just do not appear physically able to make the accent. If it does not look safe to me, they are staying on the ground.

A few times people have objected to being told to remain on the ground. Some have even insisted that this is their inspection, they are paying me, and they will climb if they choose to. They are then are told that it is my ladder and I decide who climbs it. I also tell them that I have not yet been paid for my services. I then simply and calmly explain that if they would like to play the "I'm not paying" card, I can play my trump card, called "I'm not inspecting". This is rare, but does get us all back to our proper places.

Perched Home buyer

There was a fellow a few years back who was buying a beautiful brick bungalow in an older though very trendy section of town. The home had been lovingly cared to for over fifty years. During those fifty years, the home had been added onto three different times. These various additions necessitated numerous rooflines, angles, and dormers. It all blended beautifully, but made for a very complex roof.

The home buyer had declined the offer to climb, so up I went alone. It was a wonderful roof, no sign of past repair or present need. After about fifteen minutes strolling the roof and looking out and around the neighborhood I descended, put the ladder away, and went inside to brief the buyer on the good news. The buyer was nowhere to be found.

It is not uncommon for buyers to wander around the home, usually measuring, planning their decor, and daydreaming about how wonderful life will be in their dream home. Sometimes, buyers will even go off to the store for a drink or lunch. It did not seem strange or out of the ordinary to have a missing buyer.

After finishing up the inspection in the kitchen, it was time for me to get back outside to examine the air conditioner compressor unit. As I was rounding the corner of the home's front porch, I heard my client calling to me, "Hey Wally, can you give me a hand?"

Looking around I saw no one, but looking up, I saw my home buyer perched at the peak of the porch roof! It seems he had climbed up onto the roof after denying the desire. The many peaks and valleys of the roof precluded me from noticing he had come up, or his noticing when I went down. Thankfully, no injuries or insults; just another day in the life of The Happy Home Inspector!

Get on Your Belly and Crawl!

Nothing separates the bold from the meek in the arena of home inspection participation quite like the subject of crawling in crawl spaces.

Florida is a wonderful place to live. Sunshine, beautiful beaches, and a lifestyle that most of the rest of North America can only dream of. It is the quest for that good life that attracts millions of tourists every year as well as tens of thousands of new residents. But some residents of Florida, the ones found in crawl spaces, can bring fear to the heart of even the bravest!

Traveling about the country to numerous home inspector events has provided me much in the way of education and perspective on the business of home inspecting. But whenever my peers discover I live and inspect in Florida the subject always turns to critters and creatures in crawl spaces. With their eyes the size of grapefruits, I can keep them mesmerized with my many tales. Those would be opossum tales, snake tales, and gator tales!

The way these guys are captivated by the idea of an inspector crawling on his belly under a home in Florida makes me feel like Marlin Perkins from the old television show *Wild Kingdom*. I can recall being about eight years old listening to Marlin narrate, "Jim will now wrestle the deadly 25-foot anaconda". Then Jim, dressed in khaki shorts, a shirt, and a pair of lace-up boots, would proceed into the jungle marsh to risk life and limb while Marlin kept on filming and narrating. That Jim would have made one heck of a home inspector! If he wasn't afraid of anacondas, you can bet he would be unafraid of real estate agents.

The *Wild Kingdom*

Anyway, from time to time some *Wild Kingdom*-worthy critters are lurking in crawl spaces. Most crawl spaces under houses have an access opening about two feet wide and a foot tall. Plenty of room to squeeze into, for most of us! The opening will usually then expand into a clear space measuring about two feet tall. Cool, dark, and quiet. Nice place to catch a rest and gather my thoughts midway through the inspection.

You guessed it, anything that can fit into that space has been found in that space. That would be things both living and dead. In fairness, some of the dead things never were living. Things like boards, ductwork, and trash of every sort.

Most of the dead things are not too bad, unless they are fresh; then it can be real bad! Most of the living things see or hear me coming long before I see them. They naturally head out and away from the inspector. This is a good thing and I am very appreciative that nature works this way. I'm sure the critters and I are thinking the same thing at this point—food! They think that I am coming in to eat them, and I think that they want to eat me.

It really bolsters the image of the inspector when the buyers are outside around the perimeter of the home when the critters and creatures begin to exit. Makes us look real brave; either that, or real dumb!

Much like the roof inspection, I will always ask if anyone would like to crawl on their bellies with the creatures and me. Nearly all decline. My informal data-gathering on this subject indicates to me that less than one in ten home buyers will go into the crawl space with me.

Who might you guess would be the most common type of person to venture into "The *Wild Kingdom*"? If you are thinking it's the young buck Special Forces-looking guy, you are dead wrong.

Wild Kingdom Auditions

The most common type of person that will come into the crawl space with me is a young professional woman. Show me a thirty-something woman in a blue two-piece power suit with black pumps and I'll show you someone who acts like she is on an audition for Jim's job on *Wild Kingdom*! It is beyond my skills or the scope of this book to try to describe or understand why, but that has been my experience!

One such experience in the crawl space stands out in my mind among the thousands of spaces I have crawled. The home was a typical wood frame bungalow built in the 1930s. The crawl space looked like the usual for the area. Dark, moist, and plenty of spiders. The home buyer was one who upon my first sight of her I would have bet ten to one would be a belly crawler.

I was right. Into the crawl space we went. Usually, I give my crawling assistant a flashlight of his or her own. The flashlight gives people a feeling of comfort and protection. It worked in the woods and under the covers as a ten year old, still works the same as a grown up. But in this case, only one flashlight was working, and it was mine! This situation, pitch black with only one light, necessitated that the buyer remain close by me as we entered and began to crawl. For safety, comfort, and so that she could see what I saw for easy explanation, we crawled side by side, with her left shoulder at my right hip.

As we came upon each item of interest, I would illuminate it with the flashlight while I narrated, much like my man Marlin Perkins. As I spoke, I would turn my head toward her to be sure she could hear me as well as to check to see that she understood.

During a fascinating dialog on sub-floor rot under the master bathroom, I turned my head toward her, over my right shoulder. As I was speaking to her, I felt on my left cheek something hot, wet, and rough! I screamed while in a rapid and simultaneous motion turning my head and light to see a large open mouth full of teeth only inches from my face. My motion, scream, and light scared the buyer, who now too was screaming!

So there I am, clenching the light in one hand and the buyer in the other trying to sort out what had just happened, and what would happen to us next. As I panned across the crawl, my light illuminated a large black-haired old dog, just a-smiling and wagging his tail! Seems he enjoyed the cool, dark, and quiet of the crawl space also.

When the dog saw us coming in, he just came over to greet his visitors, and give my cheek a big wet dog kiss!

Next time, I think a handshake would be preferred.

Can I Bring My Uncle Bernie?

Home inspection can be a scary time for home buyers in spite of our best efforts to make it a relaxing and enjoyable event. Usually, they love the process, but have built up some anxiety in anticipation. Many buyers would like to bring reinforcements to the inspection with them. So, what do we do now with a small army of wannabe home inspectors on the scene?

I know it's difficult to believe, but I have a few thoughts. Buyers will seek the council of friends, family members, and others whether those folks are at the home inspection or not. Many people have strong trust ties to another person or people that they consult on every decision. I see this often with Dads and daughters.

Daddy does not want anything to sadden the day of his baby girl. This is a good thing; I feel this with my own daughters. However, the problem is that Dad may know next to nothing about home buying, and almost certainly nothing about home inspecting. In some instances, Dad may have never been a homeowner! Yet, there he is, playing a key role in at least the emotional part of the purchase process and buying decision. So what to do with Daddy, and any other important guests?

My attitude is that if a person is important to a decision maker's decision process, bring them on. It is far better for all to have the benefit of the emotional support on the scene, than to have doubts created later by Daddy or others asking inane questions that frighten and confuse the buyer. How do we handle these miscellaneous inspection guests?

What to Do with Uninvited Guests

Everyone the buyer brings to the inspection party has a role to play. It is a challenge even for the expert inspector to rapidly determine who plays what role, get them into that role, and move on with the inspection, all the while maintaining the buyer's attention.

Generally, I will start one of these sessions by meeting and greeting everyone. I just want to be friendly! Then I will ask each person to explain their particular concerns about the home on behalf of their buyer buddy.

Most always, their answers will involve either something bad that happened to them or some area of expertise that they feel they possess.

What needs to happen now is that person needs to feel important and respected. This is easily accomplished in most cases. If the person had a past fearful event they dealt with in their own home, listening to their story and asking a few questions will go a long way to making them comfortable. If the person has some professional expertise or personal experience in construction or home repair, flatter that and ask them to point out any sign of problem they see in their area of interest or expertise.

Even if the total construction experience of the individual is that they once loaded drywall on trucks, let that person be in charge of drywall finish and cosmetics. After a few dozen drywall flaws are brought to the attention of the home buyer, they will soon tire of looking. Suddenly, you'll hear the buyer exclaim to the drywall guru, "It's only cosmetic!" I love it when a plan comes together!

The more difficult helper is the person who has some extremely deep level of knowledge of some technical area; it just has no relevance to home buying. One of my favorites here in Florida is a NASA engineer. When one of these detail demons gets involved in a home inspection, watch out!

It is downright comical when people of this persuasion want to answer every question with a calculator. Calculators are great, I have several, but there is no way to use a calculator to determine when a roof needs to be replaced! It might be best to assign this person the task of determining the risk of a meteorite striking the roof. That should keep them busy until the inspection is over.

Using this approach, I rarely have anyone contribute anything. Most of the guests leave within ten minutes. Nearly all whisper to the buyer that everything will be fine with this inspector. All that really needs to happen is that those people who have true and intense concern for the buyer be made to feel important. And make no mistake, they are important.

Every one of these people will play at least an emotional role, if not a definitive decision-making role in the purchasing decision of the buyer. To alarm or alienate them is to cause great stress to the buyer. This is the kind of stress that can kill deals!

I say, bring it on! Bring on the sellers. Bring on the friends. Bring on the crowds! Who knows, they might soon be in need of an agent or home inspector!

Agent Actions

The issue of agent activities at the home inspection is nearly as contentious as the issue of agents referring home inspectors. Never one to avoid a contentious issue, I will address both of these issues, beginning with agent activities.

Somewhere in time, some sage old agent told the agent masses that they need not be nor should be in attendance at the home inspection.

Balderdash, I say!

The agent has several extremely important duties to perform at this critical time. If these essential duties are recognized, embraced, and performed well, the agent will be rewarded with more deals closed, reduced liability, and a near all-referral business.

Rock the Baby

The first great responsibility of the agent at the home inspection is to do a proper and professional introduction of the home buyer to the home inspector. You must realize that most home buyers have either not purchased a home before, have not purchased a home recently, or have not purchased a similar home in the area. They are, despite any attempt at a poker face, scared!

This fear of the process is made worse when the buyer needs to go to a strange place, their wannabe home, and meet a strange person, their inspector, then go about making one of life's hardest and most expensive decisions. This fear can be greatly reduced when the agent introduces the home inspector as an experienced and familiar professional who can be trusted to guide them though the scary parts to a clear and simple understanding of the home under consideration.

Perhaps imagining the real estate deal as an infant might bring things to clarity. The deal is delicate; it must be kept warm and gently rocked. Peace and quiet is good in real estate. The hand-off of the baby from agent to inspector is a most important time. The security felt with the agent must be transferred with trust to the inspector. When the inspection is over, back the baby goes to the agent.

Please, if as an agent you do nothing else at the home inspection, get real good at introductions.

Open the Door, Please!

The next great contribution of the agent to the home inspection process is to open the door! Few home inspectors can legally obtain access to the home to be inspected, and often I question the motives of those few who do have independent access. On the flip side, the inspection never goes well if the entire inspection is conducted from the outside looking in.

While most real estate agents have access to nearly every home in the Multiple Listing Service (MLS) via a special locked box at the home containing the key to the home, very few inspectors have this access. The privilege to carry this key generally rests with agents who are members of the local real estate board. This special membership precludes inspectors from having this access. My own view is that if more inspectors had easy access to homes we would see fewer agents participating in the process. This is not a practice that I favor or find to be in the best interest of the transaction.

To Be on Time Is to Be Late

Maybe this should have been number one, but for those who need a reminder, be on time! It is an extreme professional discourtesy to be late for an appointment. Yes, I know there are circumstances that come about that make lateness unavoidable, but in my many years as a Navy pilot as well as my years as a home inspector, I always knew an hour or two in advance if "late" was to be in my future.

When the "I'm going to be late" call comes after the appointment time, no one can make up for that lost time. If you think you will be late, fess up and fess up early. When confessed early, forgiveness is easy and available with courtesy.

Having stood on the steps of a home to be inspected with many a buyer waiting for the agent to arrive, you cannot believe the things that buyers say about untimely agents. They distrust and hate this trait. What is near comical is the friendly greeting the buyer gives the agent after just having told me what a rude, lazy no good so-and-so the agent is! Go figure. I reason that buyers want to be polite even to rude agents.

Someone needs to do a study tracking agent timeliness compared with referred business and overall productivity. It is a strange phenomenon, but, new agents with low productivity seem to seldom be late, and wise and worldly tip-top producers are on time like clock-work. It is those masses in the middle that seem to muddle through the day!

Available Agents

During the body of the inspection, there is no special task of significance for the agent. Some seem to enjoy measuring and helping the buyer plan their decor, others use the time for administrative or phone contact time. What is important is that the agent be available for the buyer when emotional need or question arises.

On more than one occasion, I have watched a buyer's concern turn to comfort when an unknown was make simple for the buyer by the agent. I once came down my ladder to deliver the news to the anxious buyer that their roof was in need of immediate replacement. The buyer was nearly in tears, but she got real happy real fast when the agent explained that the purchase and sales contract stipulated that the seller would replace the roof.

Had the agent not been there, the buyer would have been a wreck during the rest of the inspection and quite possibly would have walked away from a home and deal that was ultimately good for them.

The Final Analysis

The last and final role of the agent at the home inspection is to sit in on and participate in the inspection wrap up and report review. During this period, the inspector will go over every detail of the inspection report with the buyer line by line.

If the buyer has any questions about a particular system or defect, the inspector can go with the buyer and agent directly to that item in the home. The inspector can then point out, describe, or demonstrate. This is exactly what needs to be done for a full and complete understanding of the problem and its impact on the real estate contract. This is where the agent comes in.

With the agent observing and participating in this process, many good things happen. The agent has total clarity on every element of the report and any issues that may require attention. The agent can explain if any repair money is available in the real estate contract. There is never any confusion on which item, which section, or how many of a particular problem exists. Inspector, buyer, and agent see and hear exactly the same thing. Each can tell if the other has any point in contention or confusion.

The inspection is not over until all agree on the details of every issue. Follow up calls and time spent waiting for a response or resolution go to nearly nothing. It is critical that agents participate in the report wrap up and review.

There's an Assassin in My Home!

Never should it be forgotten who owns the home being inspected. The entire inspection process can be a tense time for everyone. For sure, the buyer has nervous issues at the thought of buying a home and moving. But please do not forget the stress on the poor seller.

The seller has been in many cases bombarded by strangers snooping around their home. Even neighbors can be pests just trying to find out the asking price of the home. Everyone knows that curious neighbors capture the first batch of "for sale" flyers posted on the front lawn!

Next in the array of stresses are the many showings of the home. Ask any seller. They will tell you that it is next to nuts that they are asked to leave their home so that it can be shown to strangers. All this weighs on the mind of the seller.

When the contract, offers, counter offers, and contingencies start to fly, the seller is now near his wits end. In a sense, they are starting to feel the deal is in sight, but at the same time, the process and decision requirements are really just beginning to accelerate. Just when they thought they could endure no more, along comes The Happy Home Inspector! Nice.

It seems that the norm is to have the seller depart the scene of the inspection. I liken this to the attitude that was prevalent back in the day when expectant fathers went to the waiting room to pace until the stork arrived. Seemed like a good idea at the time, but it is now commonplace to have dad participate or at least be present in the delivery room.

Even as a man, I can see the shortcomings in my analogy, but the point is that sellers hate being sent to the waiting room! They have a vested interest in the outcome and an intense emotional desire to be there. Some sellers are concerned for the physical well being of their home, some are afraid of the tone of the disclosure, and some just want to meet, greet, and get to know the new family that is taking possession of their pride and joy.

It is beginning to sound like I am in favor of having the sellers at the home inspection. The straight answer on this is almost, sometimes, and not exactly.

The Problems with Sellers

It is important to understand and respect the concerns of the seller. They own the home and it cannot get sold without their permission and participation. They want to be there. They have every right to be there. The problems with the sellers being at the home inspection with the buyer, selling agent, and home inspector are really only two as I view it.

Problem number one with sellers at the home inspection is they often try to explain or describe too much about the home. Even though the seller may have lived the issue they are trying to disclose or explain, they seldom really understand what they are speaking about and are not professionals at disclosure during a real estate transaction. In an effort to comfort the buyer and themselves, I have watched more sellers cost themselves more repair money and kill more deals than most home inspectors could do in a whole career!

The second problem with the seller at the inspection is they distract the buyer from the inspection process.

While it is nice to know whose kids go to what school and it is interesting that the seller's second cousin once dated someone who went to third grade with Elvis, this "vital" information distracts the buyer. The buyer needs to be engaged with the home and the home inspection.

I will concede that some sellers have locked down a deal tighter then Fort Knox with their caring charm, but this is the exception.

So what to do if the seller wants to participate? Assuming that real estate agents are handling the transaction, please bring both agents to the inspection (I will get to "For Sale by Owners" in a little bit). It is very uncomfortable when both buyer and seller are together and only the selling agent is present. Aside from the ethics issues of direct contact, it can be just plain miserable to watch. And the ultimately uncomfortable thing to watch is the two agents discussing the "who said what to whose client" when situations go awry.

By practice, protocol, and ethics, agents do not speak to each other's clients without both agents being present. This is a good thing; it is one of the purposes of having an agent. But sometimes, for practical reasons, only the agent for the buyer is present at the home inspection with both buyer and seller present. In this situation, it is real hard for the agent present not to answer a direct question from the seller. Having listened to the innocence of the question and the answer, then the aftermath of both agents discussing this with each other, it is my humble but experienced position that sellers should not be at the home inspection unless their agent is also present.

Please, if the seller would like to be at the inspection, let them. But be sure both agents are present as well. Introduce the seller to both the buyer and the home inspector. Let everyone know that the seller is available to answer any question that may come up during the inspection, but have the seller go do a puzzle or weed the rose garden. It just works out better.

Finally, there is always a desire for the seller to listen in on the inspection review. This is a nice way to get everyone the same information at the same time, but few sellers can sit through this process without an unending flow of contradictions and denials. This is just not a situation in which most sellers have the temperament to participate. Best to have them start a second puzzle or another flowerbed.

Too Much Participation

Participation by everyone at the home inspection has a significance that I cannot over emphasize. The more involvement there is by everyone involved in the inspection process the better, or at least up to the point of something being damaged or a dangerous situation developing.

It is routine during inspections to run the water in tubs, sinks, and showers for nearly the entire inspection. The water is left running at just above a trickle. The constant low flow of water gives a very good indication of the waste water system's ability to relieve itself of a large quantity of water, but puts the risk of flood at a minimum. Should a stoppage occur, the last thing the inspector wants to do is spill water throughout the entire home! This fear of flooding is especially prevalent in new construction.

When scheduled to perform a new construction final inspection, we generally insist that all work be complete. It is unfair to the builder to judge the quality of work before it is complete. Likewise, if trades people are still on the job the inspection is at best a nuisance, and can often risk damage. The risk to finish work is especially high.

During one call to perform a final inspection, I arrived on the scene to discover that the home was complete, but with one small exception. Beautiful hardwood floors were being installed the living room, dining room, and throughout a large entrance foyer. The work was very near to completion with the artisans doing the final cleaning prior to the clear finish being applied. My sense was to reschedule the inspection so as not to disturb the process or risk my being the source of imperfection in what was now nearly flawless.

But the home buyer was adamant that today was the day. She had flown in from out of town just for this and it was her only chance to participate. Okay. After all, I am The Happy Home Inspector! She says move forward at any cost.

The floor finishers were not happy, but consented based on the home buyer's persuasion and my promise to take my shoes off. With an enthusiastic home buyer and an apprehensive home inspector, the inspection began.

Lights on bright, air-conditioning on full, and water trickling, the inspection was moving along great.

At least, I thought all was great.

Suddenly, I heard screaming from the floor finishers. And the real scary part about the screaming floor finishers was that they were screaming my name! Zipping at breakneck pace toward the source of the sound, I all too soon discovered the reason for the distress. Water was cascading over the top of a large garden tub in the master suite, and flowing across the tile toward those gorgeous newly-finished wood floors!

Slipping and sliding while racing to secure the water at the tub, I could not help but notice the water was not trickling out of the tub faucet, but pouring full force at a rate to rival Niagara Falls!

The floor people scattered, yelling for more rags and ripping off their shirts in an effort to get enough stuff on the floor to dam up or absorb the oncoming wave as it crossed the tile ever closer to the wood flooring in the foyer.

Now, I spent twenty years as a Navy flyer on board aircraft carriers, cruising around the globe. But the language flowing from the floor finishers would have made many a sailor blush! However, they had not yet beaten me to death. Thankfully, they were focused on the floor and not me.

We were able to stop the water before the wood floor got so much as a drop on it. The home buyer thought we were all heroes. The floor guys still thought I was an idiot, but at least they did not kill me!

Being the chivalrous character that I am, I chose not to tell the finishers that in fact it was the home buyer who had turned the tub faucets on full force!

Remember, whether you are the buyer, seller, agent, or friend, it is important for you to participate in the inspection. Walk around, ask questions, maybe measure something, but please, do not touch anything. If it is on, it is on for a purpose. If it is off, it is off for a purpose. And if it is trickling, it is for the purpose of keeping the floor people from finishing off the home inspector!

Chapter 8
Can You Find Reality in a Home Inspection Report?

At the end of an inspection, a report is generated that outlines the findings of the home inspector. This is not intended to be a "hit list" of negatives, but rather to objectively describe the home. This is not the place for emotion, rather a simple stating of the facts. Homes do not pass or fail inspections; reports merely describe a home's strengths and weaknesses.

Inspections are not intended to favor buyer or seller. In fact, the greatest flattery an inspector can receive is for the seller of a recently inspected home to call the same inspector to inspect their next home. This action tells all that the inspector discovered every defect known to the seller, and then discussed and documented those defects in a fair and objective manner. Furthermore, any unknowns discovered were likewise handled with objective fairness. This outcome should be the inspector's goal for every inspection.

For Your Eyes Only

The report provided to the home buyer by the inspector is considered to be confidential. This is a position that is at times called into question. The inspection report is always provided to the buyer. The challenge to this position comes most often from one of three sources; buyer's agent, seller, and other potential new buyers. Although these persons may seem to be legitimately interested parties, difficulties can easily arise with each.

Automatic Agent Copier

Usually, the buyer provides a copy of their inspection report to their agent. This is reasonable.

However, there have been times when the buyer has chosen to deny a copy of the report to their agent. This is rare, but this, in some situations in the mind of the buyer, seems to make sense.

A scenario where this choice has been made is when the buyer conducts the inspection prior to any offer being made. This is most common where the agent is transactional, acting on both the selling and listing side of the deal. Probably in this case the potential buyer feels that the inspection is a tool for them to decide if they desire to purchase the home, and also a tool on which to base terms and conditions of the offer.

I have also seen the buyer restrict all access to the report when the offer is for an all cash deal or an "as is" purchase. But in truth, each time in my experience the buyer has asked that the inspection report be kept from the selling agent there was the appearance of a lack of trust from buyer to agent. If, as an agent, your client chooses not to provide you a copy of their home inspection report, be wary of your position in the transaction.

The Seller's Scoop

The seller feels nearly a natural right to a copy of the report. It is, after all, their home being inspected. Then there is the issue of repairs. If the buyer seeks repairs to the home, surely the seller must have a copy of the report?

The buyer can always provide a copy of the report to the seller, but the seller has no automatic right to a copy, nor is there typically wording in the purchase and sale agreement that would compel such an action. It may be that the seller refuses a repair action absent substantiation of the problem, but even that still does not compel the buyer to provide a copy of the entire inspection report and certainly does not compel any action on the part of the inspection company.

Dead Deals and Recycled Reports

Sometimes the situation does arise that the person who contracted for the home inspection chooses not to or is unable to complete the transaction. When a new buyer is found, it is a common thought to use the previous report as a decision tool for this new buyer.

This is an extremely dangerous practice!

This is among the prime reasons that nearly all inspectors stipulate in their inspection agreement that the home inspection is considered a confidential communication between buyer and inspector.

Why do inspectors feel so strongly about this particular piece of the issue? Primarily because . . .

The written inspection report does not document the COMPLETE home inspection experience.

What? How can this be? Because, the written document only SUPPORTS the observations and dialogs exchanged by all parties at the inspection appointment. While it is certainly correct that all that is written in the report and all that is said at the inspection should be consistent, the total understanding by the buyer of the inspection comes from BLENDING the observed with the spoken and the written.

A new buyer viewing only the written portion of the inspection is missing much in the understanding, perspective, and context of the total inspection experience. This is a high-risk practice and should always be avoided.

Old Reports for New Buyers

When the original buyer leaves the transaction, generally the inspection report goes with that buyer. Because of the issues of confidentiality and, just as importantly, the completeness of understanding by the new buyer, a new inspection should be ordered.

However, in some cases, the original buyer, being the kind and decent soul that they are, will sometimes give the now "useless" report to the agent who now has another party interested in the home. How wonderful! More often, however, the original buyer of the home inspection does not know of the report handoff.

The agent and the new buyer can now use the old report as a decision tool, and all without expense. The agent is a hero to the new buyer!

Yikes! No one told the new buyer about confidentiality, or about completeness of the inspection report and experience. But, even more importantly, no one told the new buyer that there is another key reason not to engage in such a practice—things CHANGE!

An inspection report is a snapshot in time of the observable conditions of the home. That picture can change in an instant!

Things do happen to homes. Should the roof now leak or the air-conditioning now not cool, this would be an unknown to the buyer. Whether or not the seller knows is a whole other issue.

The buyer, after taking possession of the home and discovering the failure and expense to repair of failing systems, has been harmed by the lack of documentation of defect in the written inspection report. When people feel harmed, they seek relief.

When such is the case, most buyers will initially seek relief from the home inspector. Several problems exist in seeking relief from this source. Among the problems is the fact that the home inspector did not miss the failed systems, they were functioning as intended and correctly described at the time of inspection.

Next among the problems for the new buyer in seeking relief from the original inspector is that the new buyer is not the client with whom the inspector had the complete inspection experience and confidential agreement.

Nope, there is no relief forthcoming from the inspector in this situation!

Advice for Agents

So, now, where does the harmed, and getting hotter all the time, homeowner go for relief? The agent of course!

That seems rotten and unreasonable; the agent did their buyer a favor! But it was usually the real estate agent who improperly provided the previous inspection report. Worse yet, in many cases, it turns out that the complete written report was not provided, only a summary. This always goes badly for the agent!

Not only is the homeowner mad at the agent, but also the potential exists for the original buyer to discover that their report has been shared with a new buyer. If there was no permission to do this, that original buyer is typically very upset with the agent. This original buyer paid for the report and now feels betrayed by the agent. More bad news for the agent!

In a situation where the agent is still working with the original buyer for a different home than the one originally inspected, I have seen the buyer so upset with the agent that they have terminated that relationship. Strangely enough, they usually stay with the same home inspector. Relationships in real estate are about trust, and giving away someone's report is a great way to lose that trust.

So now, the agent has on one hand an aggravated homeowner that wants to be compensated, and on the other hand has just lost a potential buyer. That looks like money going out and nothing coming in! This is not a good business situation. Sharing home inspection reports with multiple clients is not a good business practice.

Ding, Ding—Round Two!

When a deal does die, the departing buyer takes the total inspection experience with them. There is nothing of use that remains other than newly discovered defects, if any, and those should be provided to the new buyer as seller disclosures.

In trying to decide who should do the home inspection for the new buyer, there are two schools of thought that give guidance on how to make that choice, or in the case of the agent, how to make that referral.

One thought is to get a second unbiased inspection from a different inspector. The thought is that a different set of eyes may see things differently, and give the transaction a fresh start.

There are certainly merits to this idea of having the inspection done by another person. Different inspectors may see things differently, document them differently, and disclose them differently. Some of these differences can be positive.

The new inspector may see something that escaped the view of the first inspector. The new inspector may have a different level of concern about an item that both inspectors saw and described in a similar way. These different views may have a seemingly positive outcome if the buyer moves forward with the deal. At least they would seem positive in the short term.

The Risk of Replacement

When a second buyer has a previously-inspected home inspected again, some of the risks of changing inspectors should be considered. To keep the thoughts simple, let us assume that both inspectors are of equal competence and that neither inspector missed any observable problems. And let us also assume, as is most often the case, the second inspector did not have access to the original report.

Not all inspectors use the same inspection format. Readers of the reports can interpret identical items reported with the same intent, differently. Something as basic as photo angles can drastically change the perspective on a problem. Just the change in report format can bring confusion or conflict into the transaction.

The greatest risk, though, is the risk of change. The original inspector knows what was seen at the original inspection and knows precisely what was intended to be read from the original report or viewed in the original photographs.

Change can take the form of material failure of a system or component. Change can also take the form of change made by the seller. This latter change is of utmost concern.

If among the reasons the original buyer chose not to complete the purchase process was a documented defect in the home, it is common that the seller will correct that item. But was it correctly properly?

If something has changed due to failure or repair, that change will be best detected by the original inspector.

Sticking Together

One of the things that makes home inspecting so challenging and exciting is trying to put a clear picture of a home together in one brief visit. That second visit some days, weeks, or months later brings amazing clarity to the inspector. It is also the best protection to the new buyer.

Try always to stay with the same inspector unless the original inspector was poorly chosen. Consistency in inspectors makes sense for all the same reasons we try to have consistency with our personal doctors.

Knowing More Is Worth More

The call to the office is a predicable one, "Wally, you inspected this house last month, the deal fell apart, can we get a discount on the re-inspection?"

Seems like a fair question—we all love discounts. At least we all love discounts when we are buyers of product or service!

Discounts are less cool when we are sellers of product or service!

But, on to the issue.

No inspector has a better shot of serving the buyer well than the same inspector who had looked at the home a month prior. There is a thought that the inspection should cost less because it takes less time. There are occasions where it does take less time, but not much less time if done correctly.

To do the inspection correctly, the entire process should be repeated again. In its entirety! The timesaving, if any, comes via a familiarity with the locations of panels, controls, and switches, not in looking at less. The reason it must be done in its entirety is because of the search for that all-elusive change. Looking for that change will always consume any time saved in familiarity with the property.

Change can be positive or negative. Something may have broken or failed. Some things may have been fixed.

If something has been fixed, has it been fixed correctly and is it now functioning as intended? To know these things requires re-examining the entire home, and redoing the inspection in its entirety.

Is this second look by the same inspector of more or less value to the home buyer? Since a second visit to the home brings such clarity to a home, clearly then the new home buyer got a more valuable service then the original buyer did! But, being the caring and compassionate kind of guy I am, I have chosen not to charge the new buyer a higher premium for the more succinct inspection.

Surely now you can see why a second inspection is worth more, and why "discount" is a dirty word!

Chapter 9
The Truth About Agents Referring Home Inspectors

Real estate agents spend a great deal of time and energy worrying about and discussing their professional liability. Having listened and participated in these sessions numerous times, I have found that one of the hottest of topics is the issue of referring a particular home inspector or home inspection company.

I am a guy who can relate to intense concerns about professional liability. It is routine to be in an exposure situation where the value of the home being inspected exceeds that inspection fee by more than 2,000 to one. This makes it absolutely vital to NOT make mistakes!

Some common agent positions on the issue are worthy of review and commentary. I have great interest in this subject, so let's discuss some of these positions.

I Don't Refer Inspectors

A position statement representative of some agents might begin with "I don't refer home inspectors because I don't want to be responsible"! This is one I hear with great frequency. Let's take a closer look at this one.

A few questions are in order. Does this agent typically refer lenders? Refer closing agents? Maybe they refer a moving company? The point is two-fold. One, agents are in the practice of referring many associated professional service providers within the framework of the transaction.

Second, and perhaps most significant, buyers are <u>expecting</u> a referral from their Realtor to all service providers needed to complete the transaction!

The agent that says, "I don't refer inspectors" ignores at least in part that the buyer WANTS the referral. At the very least, buyers want guidance and suggestions. It is not an absolute that the buyer will choose to use the referred inspector, but it is a reasonable point of reference and expectation. Remember, most buyers haven't purchased before, haven't purchased recently, or haven't purchased in the area.

Rejection of Agent's Suggestions

In some strange cases, the buyer rejects the agent's referral because it is the agent's referral! When the home buyer rejects a referral made by the agent, there are only two reasons that I have encountered. The first is that the buyer, a friend, or a family member has had a previous positive experience with another inspector. This can be a good thing. The trust from that experience most often is a benefit. But the second reason for rejection is very concerning.

If the home buyer has lost faith in the agent, the buyer may reject every suggestion of the agent. On occasion, a buyer will call our office and ask if we have ever inspected with a particular agent. When we respond in the affirmative, the buyer will thank us but reject our service stating that they no longer trust their agent and that they could never trust us if we had any history with the agent!

Why the buyer does not leave the agent is beyond my comprehension, but I can tell you, this dialog takes place more than agents realize. The truly amazing thing is that the buyer will share their distrust of the agent with the inspector, but not with the agent.

The Problem with Online Search

So, if no referral is made, how is the buyer to proceed in making a choice that provides them peace of mind? My experience is that when no agent referral is offered to the buyer, the buyer most often ends up searching online (used to be the phone book! But those days have mostly passed...). There are always plenty of options online.

Problem is, the buyer is now faced with truly boundless choices! While choice is good, boundless choice often leads to boundless confusion, or worse yet, confidence in a poor choice. Between paid search, organic search, directories, and Internet offers, it is more likely that a poor choice will be made than a proper choice.

Given the confusion caused by too many choices and no guidance on HOW to make that choice, the home buyer most often defaults to the easiest, yet least important question – price!

Price is seldom a factor in selection when homebuyers have been educated on how to choose a home inspector. They want peace of mind. Peace of mind seldom comes cheap!

How Much Should a Home Inspection Cost?

My office has had this conversation truly tens of thousands of times.

> *Ring, ring . . .*
> *"Thank you for calling HomePro Inspections, this is Tonya, how may I help you?"*
> *"Hello, how much is a home inspection?"*

This has got to be the last and least important question about a home inspection! How an agent could put their buyer, and hence their commission, in the hands of the cheapest service provider available is a never ending source of frustration and amazement for me.

This particular factor has made paid online search a magnet for only new inspectors and bottom feeders in the home inspection business. My observation is that the paid advertisements at the top of the search page are most often from the newest and least experienced companies. Their ads typically JUMP off the page, screaming their promise of being the cheapest guy around.

But did you know – a person could open a home inspection company today and buy their way to the top of paid online search results by the morning!   Not what the buyer needs; not what the agent should want.

So, how much *should* a home inspection cost? When considering the cost of the inspection, it's important to consider the value of the entire contribution of the home inspector in the due diligence process. In addition to being a decision making aid for the home buyer, there are often documents that need to be provided for the insurance company such as the 4-point insurance letter other support information that work to qualify the home buyer for insurance discounts. Here in Florida as an example, the Wind Mitigation form will often substantiate homeowner's insurance discounts.

Another document that provides peace of mind, as well as often being required by the lender, is the termite or "Wood Destroying Organism" report. Sometimes too there are comments on the appraisal that the lender requires amplification on to proceed with the mortgage. The inspector may be able to help with this documentation. Another important consideration – do you need a re-inspection of repairs at a later date? Most buyers desire any repairs completed prior to closing be re-inspected, but this is often an additional service, not included in a standard home inspection because it results in another trip to the home.

When blended together as a complete package of due diligence services, considering that most home buyers are about to commit to making 360 monthly mortgage payments over the next 30 years, it's reasonable, affordable, and comfortable to budget in the amount of one (1) mortgage payment for the complete bundle of home inspection related services. Sometimes a little more, sometimes a lot less; but using "one mortgage payment" as the measure will provide a good estimation for most homes. Peace of mind and liability management for but a single mortgage payment! THAT'S a pretty good deal.

To see a complete video presentation with specific price examples based on various size homes visit: http://youtu.be/Q75a1Kn_cUo

Remember, take actions to get quality service providers into the transaction.

The Cheap Inspection

Moving on. So, the unwary buyer invites the cheap un-experienced inspector to come do their home inspection. The agent is not familiar with the inspector; the inspector is not very familiar with home inspecting! This is a match made in heaven. More often than not this situation ends up with a very aggravated agent and a very happy buyer. How could it be that the buyer is happy and the agent aggravated?

The buyer has no reference on which to judge the inspection. The inspector was on time, neat, clean, happy, and helpful. It was a pleasant experience and they learned something. It seems good.

But the agent, having previously experienced dozens or perhaps hundreds of inspections, was not comfortable with the inspector, the inspection process, or the written inspection report. Seems the inspector made many comments about the home that the agent felt were not within what they considered the scope of the inspection. Nothing nasty or illegal; just opinions and offerings beyond the expectation.

And the inspection flow seemed different than what the agent expected. The inspector did not open the electrical panel or crawl into the attic. The inspector breezed over the plumbing. He didn't even look at the microwave!

This lack of detail was a red flag to the agent, but of no concern to the buyer. The agent is now getting very uncomfortable. Knowing that the inspector is doing a less than complete inspection, the agent must make a tough choice. Should the agent challenge the inspector? Should the agent risk scaring the buyer with the knowledge that the inspector is less than thorough, or allow the process to proceed unchecked? Is this an inspector that the agent would be comfortable with if the buyer was a family member? Things are getting scary here!

The Cheap Report

And then there's the report. The inspector did not have the ability to produce an immediate report. No worries for our intrepid agent, they just ask that the inspector e-mail the report to them. Oops! Can't e-mail the report, it's not a digital document. And oh by the way, the inspector doesn't include photos with the inspection report, either.

Two days later, the report arrives. It is in a format foreign to the agent. A call to the inspector is needed for clarification. The inspector's voice mail ensures a prompt return call. The return call comes promptly the next day!

Aggravated and frustrated with the format and difficulty in getting items explained, the agent takes issue with the urgency and magnitude of the defects described. In 15 years of experience, never has the agent had similar problems described with such veracity. The agent is certain the deal has been killed, taken out by a contract assassin!

But the buyer loves the home and buys it anyway.

The Problem with Cheap

Ten months pass. The commission check has long ago cleared. Life is good. But the phone rings and it is the now not so happy homeowner. The home is experiencing some problem.

"The home inspector should have told me about XYZ problem. If I had known, the seller would have fixed it or I would never have bought this home!"

Familiar with this scenario, the agent suggests calling the inspector for a remedy. The upset buyer informs the agent that the inspector's phone has been disconnected. The buyer does not want it to be taken personally, but please send $5,000!

Suddenly, the real estate agent wishes she had selected the inspector.

How Agents Should Refer

To begin, real estate agents should be very familiar with any state licensing issues regarding home inspectors. To refer an unlicensed inspector would be... ILLEGAL. In the wise words of Ronald Reagan – trust, then verify.

Next, confirm their experience. Not only number of years, but types of homes inspected. Full-time or part-time? How many inspections have they performed?

What about the report – what format will it be in? Is it a narrative style, or checkbox style? Does it include a minimum number of color photographs? Can it be emailed? Will it be completed the day of the inspection appointment or some number of days later?

Can the buyer or other representative be present during the appointment? Is a warranty or guarantee offered with the inspection?

Finally, will the inspector use a moisture meter, digital borescope, and infrared camera during the inspection process?

Everyone, including real estate agents, should be wary of those cheap inspectors who reject infrared technology, just as you would fear a doctor who rejects the use of an MRI or CAT scan. Those inspectors who disregard the technology are not prepared to protect anyone in the transaction – buyer, seller, or real estate agents!

Why would an agent want to refer and demand that only experienced inspectors carrying an infrared camera, borescope, and related technical tools of the profession? There are several reasons why!

Along with the home buyer gaining great peace of mind, real estate agents have gained a superb ally in the quest to manage liability. The more accurate the information provided to the home buyer, the less likely an unseen problem would result in a claim against the agent.

But more importantly, now that the technology is here, if an agent is not referring it they open themselves up to GREAT liability. Here's a scenario, one that is not far-fetched:

Sometime after moving in, the home buyer (now homeowner) has a problem. They feel harmed, rightly or wrongly. They soon learn about infrared technology and other advanced home inspection tools that may have protected them from said problem. But their home inspector didn't use any of these tools. And then they discover that their real estate agent KNEW about infrared technology, but didn't inform them about that technology. Now the homeowner feels especially harmed that their agent, the person guiding them through the home buying process, stuck them in a "money pit" just to get paid. And that is REAL BAD for the real estate agent!

Why would a real estate agent refer a home inspector who does not use this risk-reducing technology on every inspection?

The future of home inspection is here, and along with it, a new level of customer expectation is also here. It is important to us all that we learn to understand, embrace, and integrate the very best for our clients into every transaction.

Agents as Educators

It is certainly an agent's prerogative to refer or to not refer home inspectors. My own position is that it is more important to educate buyers on HOW to choose a home inspector than it is to provide a specific name.

My experience has been that agents who understand how to educate buyers in making good choices become very good themselves at choosing inspectors. What happens in this scenario is, after educating the buyer on how good choices are made, the agent then offers one or more individuals or companies that the agent has had a positive experience with in the past. It is my belief that this practice best serves the buyer, best serves the transaction, and ultimately puts the agent in the lowest-risk position. It puts the agent in a position of least risk because the agent has helped to put the buyer in the lowest-risk position!

Funny how, when the focus is the client, everything else generally falls in line!

This position of the agent as educator brings with it a level of perceived expertise by the buyer that results in trust. Trust is everything in providing professional services. That trusted referral relationship is greatly enhanced when the agent, as well as the home inspector, views their primary role and contribution to the transaction as being _educational_. If the buyer can learn from the agent HOW to make good decisions, not simply what decisions to make, things go great!

Would you like to know HOW to make great decisions when choosing a home inspector? There are secrets in the home inspection business, and some of them are dirty secrets. Most home inspectors don't want these secrets revealed, because keeping their secrets is what keeps them in business. By asking the right questions, you can be protected. The special 28-page report "The Dirty Dozen Secrets that Other Home Inspectors Don't Want You to Know" is available to you as a free bonus for purchasing this book. Just visit www.GetAHomeInspector.com

Educated buyers make better decisions that make for happy homeowners. Happy homeowners refer friends!

Chapter 10
Secrets to Reducing Risk and Delay in Real Estate Repairs

Ever wonder what the number one consumer complaint is, year after year? It just so happens that the subject of REPAIRS is always at the top of the list! To be truthful, the numbers of consumer repair complaints varies state-to-state and year-to-year between automobile repairs and home repairs. Nonetheless, the subject of repairs is always number one.

It is imperative that we, as real estate professionals, recognize that the subject of repairs is on the minds of everyone! Repairs are an essential part of almost every transaction. Repairs will continue to be a significant part of the management or ownership of every piece of property.

It is critical to our professional reputations as well as our sanity that we learn to get repairs done promptly and properly by professionals that will bring long-term satisfaction to the client. This process of getting repairs completed correctly and quickly can also be a positive reflection on the real estate professionals who referred or participated in the process.

Soliciting Repair Work

No doubt – one of the original frustrations between home inspectors and real estate agents centered on the issue of repairs. After all, following the delivery of the inspection report, an expected question from the buyer is about the repair of the discovered, disclosed, and documented discrepancies.

In the early days of home inspection this matter was aggravated even more in that many of the early home inspectors were repair contractors who did home inspections as a method of soliciting repair work.

Thankfully, this practice of using the home inspection as a tool to solicit repair work has since been deemed unethical by every state in which home inspectors are regulated, as well as by every significant inspection association. Yet, a major sticking point in the mind of many agents continues to be the whole issue of repairs.

The Three Amigos

Rules are a good thing. Rules as they relate to repairs help us to predict the outcome of the repair process. Following the Rules of Repair will lead to the highest probability of a positive outcome. These simple rules are designed to make the real estate transaction faster and easier.

It is my goal to help everyone understand the Rules of Repair, so let me begin by telling you what they are not. It is very important to know that these rules are not based in building code or statute; they have been learned the hard way! Acting outside the following rules can cause bad things to befall the transaction.

Read the rules and heed the rules.

The First Rule of Repair

There is never enough time or money to do the repair properly the first time, but always enough to do it right the second time.

Time and again, this rule raises its ugly head. The unending quest for the cheap and fast fix has gotten more people into more trouble than ever we could imagine.

Let's look at the example of some rotted sub-floor under a bathroom with two rotted floor joists.

It is very simple to do a correct and proper repair in this scenario. No need to damage the finished floor in the bathroom; the sub-floor and joists are readily accessible via the crawl space. New joists are placed the full length of the existing joists and bolted through. The sub-floor is also replaced from below and properly attached to the new joists. Fast and simple; correct and long-lasting.

But somehow, in the eternal pursuit of fast and cheap the job gets completely messed up. Most common among the errors in this scenario is the replacement joist being too short to span the entire length of the original damaged joist. This puts the old joist in the position of holding up the new joist! This does nothing to strengthen the floor.

When this "repair" is inspected, the inspector has no honest choice but to fail the repair and recommend the poor repair be ripped out so that a proper repair can be made. This always results in costs near triple what they would have been to do it right the first time. There is the cost of the poor repair, the cost to remove the poor repair, and finally the cost of the proper repair.

Then there is the issue of the time involved in this process! Fire the contractor. Bid out to several new contractors. Review the quotes. Weed through the references. Finally, choose the new contractor. Now the job must begin again! Time is simply not recoverable.

If the agent for the seller initiated this process, the seller is very unhappy with the agent. Not only did the costs triple, the time lost during the multiple visits by different repair people brings even more frustration to the transaction.

Oh, the agony!

The Second Rule of Repair

The cost of a well-done repair will be forgotten much faster than the frustration of a poorly-done repair.

Never have I heard of anyone calling his or her home inspector, agent, or repair contractor weeks or months after the completion of a well-done repair to complain about the price. It might go something like this:

> *"Joe's Siding, Joe speaking."*
> *"Joe, this is Wally. I'd like to talk about that siding job   you did for me a few weeks ago."*
> *"Are you happy with the work, Wally?"*
> *"Oh, absolutely! Love it. It's solid and looks great. And boy, were you fast and professional! I just called to complain about the price."*

This never happens! Price is forgotten fast. In fact, if the job is worthy, people will brag to their friends about how smart they are for paying more to get it done right!!

Please shop for satisfaction in workmanship and service. And you know this is especially true for home inspections.

But be certain, the calls are unending when the repair does not perform well over time regardless of the price.

Simply, price issues fade fast with satisfaction and no amount of "savings" can compensate for poor performance. If agents and inspectors truly recognized the detrimental impact on their reputations and referral base caused by their recommendation of poorly-performing repair people, we could solve this problem in a week.

It is a never ending source of amazement to me that top-producing front-line professional agents, lenders, and inspectors continue to surround themselves with budget providers of ancillary services. As your mother told you long ago, you are judged by the company you keep. To continue to refer service providers with low price as the primary priority is to continue to devalue the service of the person making the referral—that be YOU!

The Third Rule of Repair

The greatest contributor to dissatisfaction of a repair is poorly written specifications.

Suppose you call the bakery to order cake. Ring, ring, ring; hello, bakery here.

Hello bakery, I want cake.

No problem, cake on the way.

Now what the caller had in mind was a single piece of carrot cake with white icing. What the baker had in mind was a double-decker chocolate cake. It was a great cake; the recipe had won awards at major baking events around the country. The baker was justly proud of his cake, and the price reflected that pride.

When the cake was delivered the caller refused to accept delivery of the cake, telling the delivery person that he wanted cake and that to him that means carrot cake with white icing. Always wants it that way, does not like it any other way.

The baker is furious that his cake has been rejected, insulted, unpaid for, and now melted and so of no value.

Who is wrong? How did this happen?

Why is it that we would never be so foolish as to order a cake without a detailed description? No, we describe in detail our specifications of precisely how that cake is to look, its taste, its size, and in many cases, specific ingredients.

Yet, when dealing with something so complex and expensive as a home repair or renovation, it is routine to have a specification that reads only "repair bad siding". Bad move!

Let Them Eat Cake

While it certainly seems to be true that there is an ever-shrinking pool of quality repair contractors, the problem of satisfaction after the repair remains a challenge even for the best of trades people.

How can it be that honest, honorable, and experienced trades people have such a hard time satisfying seemingly bright and rational homeowners? My observation is that the key lies in the poor quality of the specification of repair.

In order to get what you want, you first need to proceed in a manner so that everyone involved in the repair process understands exactly what is desired. If we think of the repair specification as a recipe, we are real close to a complete understanding.

The Grocery List

In order to define the items of a well-written repair specification, we must think of an ingredients listing in a recipe. Let's go shopping!

The first order of business is always the item to be repaired. For discussion, the item to be repaired is "siding".

The second item of specification is the scope of the repair. In this case, the area to be repaired is stated as:

"Repair siding on left side of home, bottom three feet".

Third on the repair roster is the material to be used. For this example, "Repair siding on left side of home, bottom three feet, using 1"x6" horizontal plank siding, cut and painted to match existing siding".

And that's it. It truly is this simple!

Chapter 11
Why Do We Need Home Inspectors When We Have Building Departments?

Municipal permitting and inspections are intended to go hand and hand to ensure that safe and proper repairs are made by properly licensed professionals.

Every discussion on home inspection sooner or later comes upon the issue of building codes. Please note that "code" is a four-letter word and should be used with the same discretion that dictates your use of most other four-letter words.

The word code gets more people into more trouble in the inspection process than any other single word. A quick exercise—write the word "code" on a piece of paper. Pick up this piece of paper and read it closely. Now, wad it up and throw it away!

Remove the word code completely from your vocabulary! It can only bring trouble. It may surprise you, but I have some additional thoughts that may help sway you to never say code again.

Code Questions Rarely Are

In my experience, when an agent or home seller calls my office with a code question it is rarely *really* a code question.

Let's assume that the home inspector documented in the inspection report that "bathroom exhaust fan does not vent to the exterior". This is a common problem. The bathroom fan, in accordance with the manufacturer's instructions, must vent to an exterior space. It is commonly thought that the primary purpose of a bath fan is to remove any unpleasant orders that might be in the bathroom.

Although the bathroom exhaust fan serves this function, the fan's primary purpose is to remove moisture that accumulates in the bathroom principally from bathing and showering. The accumulation of moisture in an enclosed space often results in mold. This is the real purpose of the bathroom exhaust fan.

Now, if the moisture is extracted from the bathroom, only to be vented into the attic, we have a potentially serious problem on our hands. Imagine the warm moist air from a nice, long, hot shower being extracted from the bathroom into the attic. In almost every circumstance, the air temperature and humidity differences between the interior and attic spaces are such that when the moist air of the bathroom is vented into the attic, the moist air condenses in the attic.

It is essentially raining in the attic. This condition is perfect for the proliferation of mold in the attic. In most homes, the attic is also where the ductwork for the heating and cooling system is located. It is a certainty that the ductwork will take in some of the mold and mold spores that are floating free in the attic. The ducts then become conduits to spread the mold and spores throughout the entire home. All due to the bathroom exhaust fan not being correctly installed.

"Does the bath fan meet code?" The seller or agent when asking if the bathroom fan is required to be externally vented, is really looking for, in most cases, a reason to preclude correcting the discrepancy. Whether or not the fan meets "code" is irrelevant. The fact is, the problem caused by the fan will continue to be a problem to the homeowner regardless of the "code" requirement. Neither does the problem have to be corrected by the seller. It only needs to be disclosed. Why would someone seek a reason not to take an action to correct a defect or at least ensure that all were aware of the defect and consequences?

The Clarity of Code

The "code" is not the picture of clarity that many who seek to reference it believe it to be. In many areas, the language in the code is not terribly specific. For most installed items such as appliances, and in our example bath fans, the code almost always uses the terminology "installed in accordance with the manufacturer's instructions". This is the code writers' way of recognizing that they could never write enough code to cover every conceivable system, appliance, or installation while simultaneously recognizing the need to ensure that all systems and appliances perform safely and properly. The code writers also know that everything comes with instructions. Hence, the code people are saying, "Read the instructions".

This direction by the code writers to read the instructions seems strange since we know that men do most of these installations. We know men do not read or ask for directions. Does it really seem so strange that this is a problem?

Breaking the Code on Codes

The primary purpose of residential building codes is to set forth a minimum acceptable standard for construction. When a home is being built, it is to the minimum safe standard to meet the building code adopted by the city or town in which the home is being built. Also, when a repair or renovation alters an existing system, the item must be installed or constructed to meet current minimum code requirement.

In some situations, municipalities have mandated that particular systems, most often related to electrical systems, be made compliant with current code when a repair or renovation is made. And in more extreme instances, some municipalities have mandated such upgrades when the title to a property changes. Be sure to consult with your local building official for the particulars in your town in order to avoid any unpleasant surprises.

Whenever someone is tempted to use the "code" word, there is often an emphatic passion to its use". Is this to code?" is often posed as some great quality assurance. But in fact, what does a demand that something be built to code really mean?

Again, code is a MINIMUM acceptable standard for construction set forth by the city or town in which the home is being built. Let's break this down.

"Is this to code?" REALLY MEANS "Are you building or repairing my home to the <u>minimum</u> standard allowable by law?"

This puts the question of "code" into the perspective in which it rightfully belongs in relation to real estate sales. I don't know about you, but if code is the mini mum standard, I'd rather have my home built to the opposite of code!

More often than not when code is brought into the conversation it is the seller searching for a reason not to make a repair or the buyer displeased with the cosmetic appearance of a repair. Seldom does either of these problems have a solution based in building codes.

Stay away from using "code" as a reason for or against a repair action request.

Why Most Code Opinions Are Not

To provide even more support to the idea that "code" generally has no useful purpose in the real estate transaction, especially by the home inspector, it is important to know that only a duly authorized code official can render a code decision.

The situation with the code and home inspectors is much like the situation with the law and lawyers. Although a lawyer can certainly offer an opinion on a particular law, the judge makes the determination or interpretation. The situation with the law is so silly; we need two lawyers to disagree before a judge will even provide an interpretation. At least with code issues we do not first need lawyers to disagree, although in some situations they are the root cause of the problem.

What is important to remember is that the only person who can make a final code interpretation is the building official in the municipality in which the home is located. Home inspectors may in some cases offer an opinion, but it is in no way binding.

Likewise, be extra careful about calling in building officials to serve as a tool to cause or prevent a repair action in a real estate transaction. Once the building official is on site, you have lost complete control. There may be hot button issues in plain view of the building official that will take the property owner by complete surprise, and as we know, surprises are never good in real estate.

Remember too, that any opinion or action initiated by the building official most likely becomes public record. To have an open citation for a building code violation on file against the property that you are trying to sell is never a good thing. Do not create problems that you do not have. Leave the building officials at the permit office!

The Point and Purpose of Permits

Quick—pop quiz!

What is the purpose of a building permit?

"To raise revenue for the city or town in which the home is being built!"

Well, not exactly. While it is true that in some towns there are significant permit or impact fees associated with home building, the actual purpose of the permit process is to protect the public.

Let me say that again—the primary purpose of the permit process is to PROTECT the public.

Permit specifics vary widely, so your local building department should always be consulted before any project is begun. But some general thoughts will be of great help in sorting specifics when they come from your building department.

The permit process provides two basic safeguards to the public: plan review and contractor verification.

When a building department receives a request to permit a particular project, the plan reviewer at the building department reviews the plans of the project to ensure that the plan as depicted will result in a home being built, expanded, or repaired in a manner that will not put the occupants at risk. Often that plan review will result in the issuing of multiple permits. The permit process recognizes that many trades often need to come together to complete the project.

There may be an electrical permit for wiring upgrades, a mechanical permit for air-conditioning repairs, and a gas permit for appliance upgrades.

Each permit is specific to the trade that will be performing the work. Even the seemingly simply installation of a gas heating system with an associated electric compressor-type cooling system could become complex. This project may require multiple trades and permits to be issued. In this example, there would most likely be three permits, a gas permit, electrical permit, and mechanical permit.

My Passion

In most cases, permits can only be issued to contractors who hold the proper current license to perform the work described in the permit request. This is perhaps the greatest single benefit to the public of the permit process.

If an unlicensed or inappropriately licensed person is attempting to get a permit, the building department will not issue the permit. This screening process works great if we use the system as it was intended. But unscrupulous and illegal contractors are aware of this requirement and know how to work around the permitting system if they can get the homeowner to participate.

The issue of unlicensed contractor activity is one that I am truly passionate about. States vary in licensing law, but Florida law is very specific and very aggressive in enforcement. Be you in Florida or elsewhere, you must abide by contractor licensing laws. If all homeowners knew the laws concerning contractor licensing, the number and intensity of repair problems would drop like a rock!

Let me explain. When a homeowner is asked by the repairperson to obtain the necessary permits from the building department, it is always a red flag that something bad is about to happen. Many states are quite liberal in allowing homeowners to do their own home repairs or even construction. The same process that facilitates a homeowner doing their own repairs makes it easy for the homeowner to be improperly issued a permit for the unlicensed and dishonest contractor to perform work, or in the worst case, take the money and run without performing the work!

What About City Inspections?

The municipal building permit and building inspection process are intended to work together to ensure that the plan proceeds as permitted to a safe and proper completion. During the plan review process, periodic inspections will be specified to take place as the project proceeds. This schedule is not based on the calendar, but rather on progress. At specific points along the path of the project, the building department will be notified of the need for an inspection of the progress to that point.

These periodic inspections by the building official are performed to ensure the work has not yet been covered over by follow-on work. This gives an orderly flow to the inspection schedule so that if some defect in construction is discovered, it is as simple and inexpensive to correct as can reasonably be expected. If this schedule is followed, the properly executed work does not need to be disturbed to correct some deficient work that came before it.

When the municipal permit and inspection process is honored and executed properly, it gives the project the highest probability of a positive outcome with the lowest risk to both safety and expense to the consumer. Any attempt to shortcut or defraud the process is always looking for trouble.

Chapter 12

Is This a Home Inspection or Crime Scene Investigation?

Home inspection is not just for home buyers anymore. There are an ever-increasing number of uses for the expertise a home inspector has to offer. While the pre-purchase home inspection remains the most popular type of inspection, there are many other times that a home inspector can provide valuable insight and objectivity to a situation. Examples:

1. The best time to inspect

2. Pre-settlement inspections

3. Partial inspections

4. Property management inspections

1. The Best Time to Inspect

A home inspection conducted prior to a home being placed on the market is one of the wisest moves a seller can make. But often the initial response from sellers when approached with the idea of an inspection done as the home is about to be put up for sale is most always the same—"What?!"

Let's review a few of the most common concerns about Pre-Listing Home Inspections.

Fear of Inspection Rejection

"The buyer will not accept an inspection done for the seller".

That is correct! The inspection done for the seller is not intended to replace the inspection done for the buyer. The purpose of the pre-listing inspection is to put the seller in control!

Given that no good surprise can come to the seller during the home inspection, regardless of when it is done or whom it is done for, it makes perfect sense to get every strand of information as soon as it can be gotten. Bad news doesn't get better with time.

If there is some bad news, or more correctly, some items that need attention or might have an impact on the home's value, who better to receive that information than the seller? And when is a better time to receive that information than before the home is placed on the market?

The simple fact is this—a home inspection before listing will put the seller in the best possible position. With a complete and clear view of the home's strengths and weaknesses, the home can be marketed to the best benefit of the seller.

Want Not, Pay Not

"I don't want to pay for the inspection".

This is certainly understandable. The seller generally perceives that the inspection is intended for the buyer; hence, it should be a buyer's responsibility. But to have the benefit of the information, it must be paid for. Never have we had a complaint from a seller about the value of the inspection! In every case at the conclusion of a pre-listing inspection, the seller felt they had made a good choice in spending the money to get the inspection done.

In most cases, the sellers feel good getting the peace of mind of knowing that no major event or expensive issue will be uncovered by the buyer's inspector. And on the rare occasion when it is discovered that the roof is completely shot or there is some other big expense or danger, the sellers, while not happy to have the problem, are glad to have discovered it on their own terms. The small expense of the inspection is always less than the cost and aggravation of a hurried hunt to get something repaired or replaced after the home is under contract.

Save the pain, spend the money. Get every home inspected prior to putting it on the market.

It Is as It Be

"The home is selling 'as is'".

This may be the best reason of all to inspect at listing! If the home is being sold "as is," reduce your risk and liability as the seller by getting a pre-listing inspection. In order for the home to sell quickly and at the highest price, disclose every condition of the home. The inspection gives both the buyer and the seller the comfort of knowing that the home "is as it is". With a pre-listing inspection, there is a high likelihood that the home IS as represented.

Even in an "as is" contract, the buyers may still have their own inspection performed. If these two inspections are similar in content, it is rare the buyer will walk or counter offer. That, in fact, is the goal of the "as is" sale.

Seller Repairs

Sellers are often concerned that every item discovered to be problematic on the inspection report needs to be repaired.

This is simply not true. It would be true that every problematic item needs to be disclosed, and those disclosures may impact value and hence asking price, but nothing need necessarily be corrected.

Amazing as it may seem, homes inspected prior to going on the market have two very significant attributes:

1. **They sell faster** than homes not inspected until the buyer has made an offer.

2. **They sell closer to the asking price** than homes not inspected until the buyer has made an offer.

Why the heck does this happen?

Why Buyers Pay More and Faster

When the buyer makes an offer, there is an assumption made by the buyer, reasonable or not, that there is nothing wrong with the home! If there was something wrong with the home that the seller knew about, but did not disclose, shame on them—it is about to cost them money. Most often, though, the items that come up on the inspection by the buyer were unknown to the seller.

Sur-prise, sur-prise, sur-prise! And we've already established that surprise is not good in real estate. So how is it that the inspection for the seller makes the buyer pay more for the home and do it in less time?

Let us create an example of a 20-year-old home that has a fair market value of $100,000, just to make the math easy. That value assumes that nothing is wrong with the home. When the buyer has the home inspected it is with the assumption that anything discovered to be wrong will be corrected by the seller or a price concession will be made.

Now, let's consider that the buyer's inspection revealed the need for a new roof, several plumbing leaks, and the need for replacement of three exterior doors. When these discoveries are made by the buyer's inspection, the clock is running and running fast. These items need to be corrected before the sale can be completed. This time crunch puts the seller at a disadvantage when dealing with the contractors.

When time is critical, you have fewer choices and the costs go up. Additionally, the buyer often wants to have input on WHOM does what work.

This situation is always tense and expensive. But it can be avoided!

Let us now assume that an inspection shows the same results, but it is for the seller before the home goes onto the market. The seller is now in control. Armed with a clear picture of what is wrong, the seller can choose to shop calmly for the best value in repair contractors, offer a credit at closing, or adjust the sale price to reflect the diminished value.

No matter the choices made, the seller, on the seller's time frame, makes them. This actually makes for a neater, simpler buying decision for the buyer. The buyer knows better what condition the home is in and knows what issues to base the initial offer on.

The buyer will still in most cases get the home inspected, but it is a breeze. It is rare that any additional items of significance arise. The pre-listing inspection puts deal killing at the lowest risk. Most often, it makes for a deal-closing tool!

2. The Buyer's Last Chance

Prior to taking ownership of a home, the last opportunity to examine the home is the Pre-Settlement Walk-Through, sometimes called a final walk-through. The home buyer, while accompanied by their agent, usually conducts this inspection.

At times, due to the complexity of repairs, the buyer may elect to hire a home inspector to also participate in this final walk-through. If the decision to hire an inspector is made, every effort should be made to have the same inspector that did the original pre-purchase inspection. To bring in a different inspector at this late date is to increase the likelihood of confusion.

Another time when a professional inspector might be brought in to conduct the pre-settlement inspection is if the buyer is unable to be at the inspection themselves. On occasion, this duty has been dumped on the agent.

This is not a good place for the agent to be. The agent seldom knows the mind of the buyer well enough to make such a large decision, and the agent rarely has the technical skills to protect the buyer's interest properly.

The blend of high buyer anxiety when absent, combined with a lesser set of technical skills than the professional inspector puts the agent in an extremely high-liability risk position. Agents should avoid being the sole decision maker in pre-settlement inspections.

Well, why is it that there would need to be a pre-settlement inspection? There has been, in most cases, a previous professional home inspection. The simple answer . . . things CHANGE!

The Search Is On!

The initial and most obvious change is that during the pre-settlement inspection the home is vacant. More often than not during the original pre-purchase inspection, the home was still occupied by the seller. In addition to the furnishings and wall hangings, most sellers begin packing for the move about the time of the inspection. These beds, bookcases, and boxes all restrict the inspector's ability to observe the home. When the home is empty, you may observe things that no one has seen in years.

Sometimes during the move-out process, the seller will make an unpleasant discovery. Perhaps the dresser in the master bedroom blocked the observation of a leak in the adjacent master shower stall. No one knew! The inspector could not see this area to detect the stain.

Moving such pieces of furniture does not happen during a home inspection. The seller was unaware until the moving company was loading the dresser.

Surely, in this situation any honest seller would get this information immediately to the buyer via their agents. But, I am sad to report, sometimes people lack the integrity to do the right thing. Or worse yet, they may take an action to mask the symptom from the buyer without correcting the cause of the problem. This spells double trouble for the buyer. The problem will continue to worsen after they move in, undetected until it is ugly and expensive to correct.

Sometimes too, the seller acts in good faith to repair the newly discovered problem, but lacks the skill to do it well. Though not a dishonorable act, it has the same impact on the buyer as if it was done with the intent to deceive. Then too, when the buyer does discover the now worsening problem, they virtually always find it difficult to believe that the seller had the interest of the buyer in mind if they did not disclose the discovery of the problem prior to closing.

Be diligent during the pre-settlement inspection! A common change is that fixtures or furnishings that were to be included in the sale of the home are now missing. It is not uncommon for a dining room light fixture that was in the home at the original inspection to have been removed to live again with the seller. More difficult to spot is when a light fixture is completely replaced. Sometimes these situations are honest miscommunications, and at other times these actions are made with not-so-honorable intentions.

Researching Repairs

Another important reason to perform a thorough pre-settlement walk-through is to confirm the completion and proper performance of repairs that should have already been done. Be sure to compare the original repair request with the invoice for work and to the look and function of the repair. If need be, have the repair contractor assist with this inspection.

Check to see if warranties and guarantees are in the name of the buyer. Often a seller becomes the client of the repair contractor and the warranties do not transfer. It is very upsetting to the new homeowner with a complaint or problem when the contractor tells them that the warranty is not transferable. This is especially aggravating when the system, component, or appliance was never even operated by the seller!

No One's Fault

The condition of the home can even change without anyone having taken any action. Nature has a way of treating vacant houses cruelly. Limbs fall, wind blows, and rain pours. All of these can have a damaging effect on the home.

Sometimes the damage to the home is done by the home itself. Pipes break, appliances fail, and wires do catch fire. It is up to and the ultimate responsibility of the home buyer to be sure that the home looks and functions as it should.

The point is, the strangest things can happen between the inspection and the closing. One of the strangest I ever encountered was with the help of the local utility company. The water had been turned on in a vacant home to allow for the home inspection. The inspection revealed a problem with the water heater. A day or so after the inspection, the water was again turned off by the utility company.

A plumber was contracted to replace the water heater, all work to be completed and paid for at the time of settlement. The plumber was fast in starting the job. The old water heater was removed, but before installation of the new water heater was completed, the plumber was called away to another more urgent job. This was the day before settlement.

On the morning of settlement, the utility company did as they were asked and turned the water back on. This resulted in water flowing throughout the entire home for most of the day until the home buyers came for the walk-thru inspection! Needless to say, the closing did not happen on time! Had the buyers not done the pre-settlement inspection, their first night in their new home would have been soggy!

Ultimately, the pre-settlement inspection is the buyer's last chance to protect themselves from the risks posed by the home before they do in fact own it, risks and all.

3. That's an Incomplete!

Frequently, we get a request in the office for a "Partial" Inspection. This is another of those things that truly escapes my logic. While I am sure that the basis for this request is the desire to reduce the expense of the inspection, partial inspections are bad for everyone.

Let me tell you why!

The most common partial inspection request is for a roof inspection. People are always worried about the roof; primarily due to the high replacement cost and the probability of extensive damage to the interior of the home should the roof fail.

Here's where the problems begin. Most folks assume that the roof inspection takes place on the roof. It is certainly true that walking on the roof is an element of the roof inspection. But to really judge the past history and future expectation of the roof, the interior of the home as well as attic space should be likewise walked, or crawled.

By inspecting the interior of the home, viewing the ceilings, we can often see signs of past water intrusion.

Stains are the home inspector's friends! They tell the history of past performance. Likewise, ceiling patch or paintwork can be indicative of past or present leak issues. We need to look at the entirety of the interior to best assess the roof.

Moving on to the attic. The tale is really told here. More often than not, roofs leak for quite some time into the attic before the leak is detected in the interior living space. Some leaks begin so small that for years the wood roof decking is kept wet and rotting. This is most often discovered when the roof is removed and replaced. This is when the roofer delivers the unpleasant news that there is a significant additional expense above the quoted price due to the need to replace many sheets of rotted roof sheathing.

Home inspectors get their most important information about past and present roof risks from the attic. The attic must be viewed in total to properly assess roof performance.

The Problem with Partials

Okay, you say, so the roof inspection involves other areas of the home. What's the issue? Well, the problem becomes that during the interior and attic portions of the inspection it usually happens that additional issues are observed. Let's keep the example tight.

During the interior inspection, no signs of roof leak were detected and no additional concerns for any other system were observed. But while in the attic, an active roof leak was detected. There was rot to the roof sheathing. Also, water had been dripping onto the ductwork in the attic. The ductwork was metal and had rusted through in some areas. Mold was observed to be growing in the ductwork.

In addition, water was dripping onto the main service electrical wire that leads to the main electrical panel. It could be seen that water had been getting into the panel and much rust and corrosion had taken place. This is a dangerous situation. It necessitates immediate correction to keep the home and family safe from shock and fire.

Now the complication becomes that we are supposed to be inspecting the roof. How does this newfound information get disclosed to both buyer and seller? And what if a roofer, and not a home inspector, had conducted the partial inspection for the roof? Would the roofer even be able to recognize the other great dangers?

Most likely not.

The problem with partial inspections is that no system operates, or fails to operate, in a home without some interaction or impact on other systems in the home. To view a system without respect and consideration of the interaction of all related systems is to not properly inspect the system.

Avoid partial inspections at all cost. It is bad for the home buyer, home seller, agent, and inspector alike. Frankly, I view with suspicion any home inspector who performs partial inspections during the purchase and sale process.

4. Property Managers and Landlords

It is becoming ever more popular to have home inspectors involved with property managers and landlords in assisting with building information for maintenance budgeting and liability management.

Maintenance costs are a fact of home ownership. When a landlord or property manager is faced with predicting and accounting for these costs, a home inspector can be of great use. Of course, the inspector can assist initially in the purchase process, but that should only be the beginning of the relationship.

The home inspector can provide annual check-ups of the property's condition. Often there is an uncomfortable tension between landlord and tenant. The home inspector can bring an objective perspective to the mix.

Input from the tenant can provide insight into the home's strengths and weaknesses that in some areas go beyond the inspector's ability to observe during a home inspection. When the tenants all-day-every-day observations are combined with the inspector's expertise, the clearest possible picture of the home can be seen.

This crisp picture of the home's condition and performance allow the inspector to help the landlord or property manager craft a cost-effective maintenance plan. In addition to the periodic maintenance plan, this approach allows long-term expense predictions to factor into budgeting.

The home inspector can also be used to review repair specifications. When confronted with multiple and dissimilar bids for a renovation or repair, the home inspector can help sort the options and differences so that the choices seem simpler.

A last role that the home inspector can play is in helping to sort tenant complaints. Often a tenant will be unhappy with some aspect of the home's condition or performance. If the source or magnitude of the problem is unclear, or the landlord does not feel there is basis for the complaint, the home inspector can again provide that objective perspective to bring the parties to consensus.

Shock the Assassin!

I once had an interesting call from a property manager who was trying to solve a tenant's complaint. It seems the tenant was upset that the driveway and parking area behind the building had on more than one occasion cut the feet of their six-year-old while he was barefoot. Barefoot kids and banged up feet are a regular part of life in Florida. But feet getting cut while simply walking across a driveway is a situation out of the ordinary! The property owner went to visit the location and observed the drive to be made of pieces of a coarse, brittle material, but was unsure of its type or source. I was asked to have a look.

The building was an eight-unit two-story brick building, probably constructed in the 1930s. It was attractive and appeared well cared for. When I saw the driveway, I was in shock. The driveway and parking lot were composed of crushed asbestos roofing shingles!

Most of the homes in the area of this building originally had asbestos roofing shingles; most had been removed over time. When this particular building was re-roofed, the roofer made the horrible decision to use the asbestos material for the driveway and parking area.

Not a good or legal choice!

The property manager was horrified. The liability exposure for the property manager probably posed a greater risk to the management company than the asbestos did to the tenants! The property manager and the property owner had some serious issues to address, but at least they were in a position to solve those issues before the lawyers and EPA got involved.

Chapter 13
Should Brand New Homes be Inspected?

Most of us have had the experience of purchasing a new car. Who among us has made that new car purchase and not had to return the car to the dealer for some reason within the first month of ownership? This practice has become so routine that it is essentially an expectation that we will return the vehicle for some reason or another.

Why then, if we expect to have return needs for a highly refined machine, built by robots in a controlled environment, would we expect that a home, built entirely by humans in an outdoor environment, would not have some built-in problems?

The Power of the Phaser

Of course, things will go wrong. Most often, they are minor, but the scary thing is that all too often the problems take months or even years to show any symptoms.

In the time before the appearance of symptoms, it is common that great damage can occur. This is the case with moisture intrusion, which can often lead to mold problems (see our resource page at http://www.somedaypublishing.com for more information on mold and moisture).

Another great risk is that a symptom will not show itself until after the builder's warranty has expired. This can be a fabulous frustration and expense. The source of the problem can clearly be traced to a construction flaw, but because of the time lapse from construction-defect to defect-discovery, the homeowner is left holding the bag. And this situation is usually not covered by a homeowner's insurance policy.

Some latent defects caused by a builder may go undetected for decades. Often the home has functioned fine for years, but in the course of opening a wall during a renovation or rebuilding a portion of the home after a fire, the walls are open and a defect that had no symptom is observed. These events are rare, but they do happen.

How then can this risk be avoided or reduced? Inspections of new homes are the answer and more specifically, Phased Inspections during the construction process.

Phaser Frequency

The frequency of phase inspections is a value judgment. The expense to have a private home inspector monitoring construction on a daily basis is beyond the affordability of most buyers. But, by inspecting at key times during construction, the benefit of inspection can be blended with a value decision. This not only brings the comfort and protection desired by the buyer, but does not break the bank in the process.

Those key inspections are: the foundation or pre-slab, framing, pre-drywall, and the final inspections. Inspections during these key phases give the inspector the best chance of detecting any deficiency since the principal points of concern during each phase remain visible to the inspector.

It's All About the Timing

I cannot stress how important it is to schedule and coordinate phase inspections, allowing the inspector to view the project at the proper time. Some inspections can only be done at very specific times in the construction process. An important example is the pre-slab inspection.

On homes that are built on a concrete slab, it is vital to view the project just as the slab is ready to be poured. The area beneath the slab is critical. There are pipes, electrical conduit, and vapor barriers, to name but a few important items to be observed. Once the concrete slab is poured, these components are buried forever, never to be seen again. Likewise, if the inspection is scheduled too soon, they are not yet in place.

We get numerous calls into the office asking if we can still do the pre-slab inspection after the concrete has been poured. Yes, we can look at the slab, but the chance to see a problem is greatly reduced and the cost to correct defects has gone up considerably. Timing is everything in new construction phase inspections.

It is also important to schedule these inspections to allow enough time for the builder to respond to and correct defects. When any phase inspection is omitted, it reduces the likelihood of defect detection, and increases the expense to correct as construction moves along.

Happy Birthday, Baby!

A fifth very important, though often overlooked, type of new construction inspection is the One-Year Warranty inspection. Performed when the home is 10 or 11 months old, the purpose of the one-year warranty inspection is to evaluate the condition of the home prior to the expiration of the builder's warranty.

There is a tendency during the one-year builder's warranty to focus on the thought that it is the last chance to beat up on the builder before the entire responsibility of the home is transferred to the homeowner. But, there are concerns other than poor builder performance.

Did the Builder Perform?

Of course, the first concern during one-year warranty inspections is builder performance, looking for anything done improperly during construction.

If the home had phase inspections during construction, it is rare to discover a builder-induced defect at the one-year point. When there are defects or problems discovered at this point they are usually minor, usually moisture related, and often both.

Minor moisture problems discovered in a timely manner are generally simple to solve. Major or long-term moisture problems often result in significant structural problems and on occasion, significant mold problems. Of all the experiences you do not want to have in a home, major mold remediation has got to be near the top of the list.

A subset of builder defect is the manufacturer's defect of installed material, systems, or appliances. Through no fault of the builder, a bad batch of roofing shingles may have been used on your roof. Even if perfectly installed, these shingles will have a higher failure rate and greatly reduced life. Likewise, a well-installed appliance may be in the early stages of failure or the subject of a manufacturer's recall. Though not the fault of the builder, it is important to make these discoveries as soon as possible so as not to void a warranty or miss an opportunity to be compensated for the defective item.

Significant Events

The second source of problems is event related. Some physical damage has occurred to some component or system of the home during its short life. Tree limbs damaging siding, wind tearing roof shingles, and pets ripping screens would be common examples. None of this type would be a builder responsibility to repair, but important to repair immediately to prevent additional damage to the home.

It is important to get these items corrected even if it means an out-of-pocket expense to the homeowner. Sometimes, the homeowner may be fortunate enough to have the damage be a covered peril under their homeowners insurance.

Never Needs Care

The third source of discrepancy often discovered during the warranty inspection is maintenance items. These are those periodically recurring events such as changing air filters, caulking bath tile, and cleaning gutters.

All of the items in this class are the responsibility of the homeowner. Many of these seemingly small and insignificant items, if left unchecked, can result in major expense as more damage is done. Additionally, poor care leads to reduced life of equipment and appliances. It is time and money well spent to participate with your home inspector to learn as much as possible about long term care and preventative maintenance of your home.

Romancing the Builder

Being a homebuilder is among the most respected and revered professions. If home ownership is truly the American Dream, then homebuilders are Dream Makers! The business of home building certainly can have its rewards. Done well, it can make a person among the wealthiest and most successful and admired members of the community. But home building is a challenging and ever-changing business.

The competition among builders is fierce. The competitive position for buyers is intense, but far from the greatest challenge in many parts of the country. The shortage of skilled trades people has driven up costs and, some would argue, driven down quality. These escalating costs, coupled with the limited availability of workers, contribute to rising home prices and scheduling problems. In many locales, the scarcity of buildable lots is a critical issue. Finally, the transition of home building from small local builders to publicly traded companies operating on a national scale has changed the landscape of homebuilding immensely.

On top of all this, here comes the home inspector!

My Inspector and Hairdresser

In trying to provide a better service to our client, the new home buyer, a large amount of my time and energy has gone into trying to understand why builders resist, and in some cases plain dislike, home inspectors. Much can be learned by listening. It is worth hearing some common builder comments, then providing some commentary.

Builders have been heard to say, "If you knew how to build, you'd be a builder"!

This is a fair and reasonable thought. In the early years of home inspecting, nearly all home inspectors were builders or remodelers. These folks came to home inspection rather by chance. Someone from their existing client base would call to ask the builder or remodeler to "check out a house" they were about to buy. Or on occasion, check on the progress or resolve an issue with their current builder. That was fine.

Over time, however, home inspectors have begun to come from professions unrelated to building or remodeling, or even construction at all. I even know an inspector whose previous job was cutting hair and selling shampoo!

Many of these people have studied hard and educated themselves well.

They are superb home inspectors. Many others do it rather poorly. And some do very well with the inspection of re-sale homes, but lack the specific expertise or experience to do phase inspections during new home construction.

The builder's comment seems at least reasonable. A home inspector who had a solid background in new home construction would have, among other benefits, a more credible position with the builder or the builder's superintendent.

Feeling Official

Another common builder comment: "If you knew anything about building codes, you'd be a building code official"!

Again, not a completely unreasonable thought. One of the shortcomings of this thought, though, is that many builders do not believe that building officials know much about building, or much like the home inspectors, they too would be builders!

Another problem with this builder comment is that the building official's charge is to ensure the home is being built to the standard of the code, which, by its very design, is a minimum. If more new home buyers and agents recognized the minimalist nature of building codes they would be much less likely to banter the "code" word about as though it were gospel.

If home inspectors and municipal building inspectors were looking only at the same things and from the same perspective, the builder's comment would be closer to target. But this is simply not how it works. Home inspectors spend more time, looking at more issues, from more perspectives than those charged to the building official. My offering is that when properly performed, each type of inspection complements the others in helping the home to be the best that it can be.

Wrongly Accused

And it was also heard: "You tell my client I am wrong"!

Yes, sometimes things do get done wrong. This is most often in spite of the best intentions and actions of the builders. Sub-contractors do at times let builders down, building officials do miss things, and sometimes an act of nature or a vandal does something to mess up the process.

If something wrong is discovered during the building process, it is best for everyone involved to make the discovery, and make it as soon as possible. As time goes by, the problem will surely worsen, be more expensive to correct, and/or be more difficult to locate. The only better time to discover a problem than now is to discover it yesterday.

Simply informing the buyer of something done wrong isn't done to point fingers, only to put the buyer in the most informed position. Pointing fingers at *any specific person or organization* is not the desire of the home inspector.

One goal of the inspection is to assist the builder in discovering any situation or defect in the home that might result in an unhappy buyer. Some of the discoveries made are downright dangerous! For example, tools have been found left in electrical panels and heating systems. These dangers can pose a huge liability risk to the builder should an injury occur. To impede the home inspector is to increase the builder's liability.

Often, too, the builder has sub-contracted portions of the work to trades people. If a sub-contractor has performed poorly or has not completed work, the home inspection report can be used by the builder to objectively substantiate this poor performance.

A well trained, credentialed, and experienced home inspector can be a great asset to a homebuilder when both view the goal of client satisfaction as one in common, not in conflict. Many builders are beginning to not only suggest private home inspections to their clients, but in some cases will share in the expense!

I love a progressive mind!

The Generation Gap

And my favorite builder comment is, "I do it the way I have always done it, just like my Daddy and his Daddy who started this company"!

You have got to respect tradition and longevity. But, two big issues come to mind. The first is, "Have you, Pappy, and Grand Pappy always done it wrong?" The comment that it has always been this way sometimes, in fairness, means it has always been done incorrectly.

The second issue is that some things do change. Building codes change, building materials change, and sometimes a better, simpler, faster, cheaper, or easier idea does come along. It is okay to change if change makes sense and is a change for the better.

Are Buyers Wrong?

As many times as not, the home inspector is telling the new home buyer that they, the home buyer, are wrong. People watching their own home being built is much like watching one's own surgery. It is real messy, real scary, and often painful. Sometimes just the fear of it all makes buyers uncomfortable, so they see or feel problems that are not problems.

Among the most common problems that are not problems are "knots". If I had a dime for every time someone called the office in a panic because their builder used a stud with a knot in it, well I would not need to write books to fund my retirement! Buyers need the comfort of an objective expert opinion to confirm for them that their builder is doing a fine job and that any defect discovered will be brought to their attention for resolution.

That still does not make every builder in town happy to have their work inspected, but it sure does make new home buyers happy!

New Home Final Walk Through

Before taking possession of a new home it is every bit as important to do a complete walk-through inspection as it would be if the home were one hundred years old. This inspection is the perfect time to learn how to operate the home as well as to detect any items or installations that might need repair or correction prior to the closing.

The National Association of Home Builders (NAHB) suggests four important purposes for the buyer's final walk-through inspection.

First, the inspection is a time for the buyer to learn how to operate the home. Much like when buying a new car, switches are in different places and some of the gadgets and gizmos that were intended to make life simple, can actually complicate life if not completely understood. Some appliances and systems can be dangerous if operated incorrectly.

Second, during the final inspection, the home buyer will learn of the maintenance responsibilities that they as homeowners must take on. No matter how fine the home is built or how durable the materials, if the homeowner does not perform proper periodic care, house failure and the associated expense are sure to follow. And sometimes follow fast.

Third, most all homes come with a builder's warranty. The common length of term is one year. The builder can detail the covered areas as well as the procedures to file a claim. It is important that all claims or complaints with a builder are always in writing. This gives the builder the best chance to please the homeowner. It also gives the new homeowner the most recourse if the builder does not please.

And fourth, the final walk-through inspection gives the builder the chance to share their knowledge of the larger community with the homeowner. Often the developer has provided numerous community amenities, such as pools, parks, and playgrounds that will now be available to the family. Some of these will have additional fees while others will be accessible merely for buying in the particular community. The builder will be able to explain all of these opportunities.

Committed Builders

Probably my best example of a builder's commitment to involving the home inspector to deliver the best home to a satisfied home buyer occurred a few years ago. Upon arrival at the home, the builder and his superintendent greeted me. The builder appeared truly glad to see me, even had an extra cup of fresh Starbucks coffee for me! Wow, I was getting happy, but suspicious. Did he have the intention of killing the deal killer?

The builder said that he and the superintendent had prepared a final list of items to be corrected in the home. The builder asked that I take all the time needed, go over the home with a fine-tooth comb, and then we would compare and combine lists! I was getting weak in the knees! Could it really be that rather than fear, fight, or oppose the inspector, there was another who saw us as all working together?

When my inspection was completed, I summoned the superintendent for the list merging. The process of blending the lists revealed that some items had escaped the view of the builder, and in fairness, they showed an item or two that I had not discovered. We each had validated the need for each other, and especially the need to work together.

It goes without saying that the home buyer was truly thrilled by the team approach. Life is just better when we play as a team!

The Cat in the Attic

Strange and unexpected things do happen during home inspections. Seldom are they tragic, often they are humorous. Not long ago, one of our inspectors was performing a new home final walk through inspection.

Accompanying our inspector were the home buyers and the builder's superintendent. As the superintendent was explaining the many and varied features of the windows, our intrepid inspector went into the attic to have a look around.

While in the far reaches of the attic, with light shining bright, the unmistakable reflection of eyes was observed. As he went closer in an attempt to identify the eyes, not by name or color, just critter classification, the critter made a dash out of the light. As our inspector followed the dashing fur ball, it became clear it was a cat. After some time spent trying to encourage the cat toward the attic pull-down steps, our inspector, not being a cat herder, descended the steps to tell the superintendent of the problem.

The superintendent went into the attic, scanned and panned, but saw nothing. The home buyers were somewhat amused, but did not want a cat in the attic. On the compassionate side, the cat could not live long in an enclosed attic. On the practical side, if the cat were to die somewhere in the attic, well-baked cat does not smell very good! The home buyers would not accept the home unless the cat was removed.

The superintendent was not a happy guy. However, he took responsibility for the situation and called a local trapper to capture and release the cat. It seemed like a good solution for everyone, including the cat.

When the cat-catcher arrived, things were looking up. He seemed like a gentle man who would rescue the kitty and everyone would live happily ever after.

It was not so easy. Cat man could not find the cat. After an hour of meowing, here kitty-kitty-ing, and other cat-catcher techniques, the cat was nowhere to be found.

This seemed like a reasonable outcome. Cat out of attic, happy home buyer, happy cat. But things are never simple.

Cat man gave his invoice to the builder's superintendent. It was for $95. Cat hunters are paid quite well! Anyway, the superintendent refused to pay the bill since the cat catcher did not catch a cat. The cat hunter departed, madder than a wet cat, hissing all the way back to the office.

Chapter 14
And In Closing I'd Like to Say……

And so here we are together, author and reader, getting ready for the close. We are in a situation similar to those that I find myself in every day with home buyers. We have journeyed along an information path, but to what end?

For the home buyer, that end is a buying decision. It is a big decision with huge consequence if poorly made.

And for the buyer, no matter their decision, it brings the need for more decisions.

If the decision is "buy," then any deficiencies discovered during the inspection must be distilled down to a repair or negotiation list, commonly some of both.

If the decision is "pass," then every decision previously made to get to that point must be made again for the next home. For some, sadly, the "pass" decision causes such stress that it becomes a pass on home ownership. This is a tragic end to a dream, and it truly saddens me.

Helping buyers, sellers, and agents to get the deal done was a prime motivator in the decision to write this book. It is a personal loss I share with every buyer when a deal has died, because with it, if even just for the moment, the dream has died.

Those inspectors who find some sick source of professional pride in the "Deal Killer" label truly distress me. Why anyone would want to seek out reasons for someone not to buy a home is beyond me. "Deal Closer" should be the title that is revered!

I firmly believe that an inspector can earn reverence only by helping and educating home buyers to fully understand their prospective homes. If buyers are fully aware of the risks and remedies, the costs and consequences, the pitfalls and potential of their future home, they can make decisions that are right for them. These are decisions seldom regretted. That is the role of the home inspector.

Having said and shared so much about the use of home inspectors, one question still remains, "What do I do with this information?" What to do depends on who you are.

So What's a Buyer to Do?

Every buyer of every home should have a home inspection.

There are few calls to me that are more distressing than those from a homeowner in a desperate financial fix brought on by an unknown problem with an un-inspected home.

The most distressing among those is from the new home buyer who cannot believe that the builder and building officials are nowhere to be found when it is time to solve legitimate problems. Certainly this is not the situation with every new home, every builder, or every building department, but I am here to tell you that it happens often enough that I am never surprised by the call. I'm only surprised by the fact that the calls continue to come!

The buyer should be at the inspection to ask any and every question on their mind. The unasked question is always the one that comes back to haunt! It is especially haunting when one person had the question and another person suppressed or dismissed the question as frivolous or unimportant.

If questions remain at the end of the inspection that are beyond the ability of the inspector to answer, or even beyond the scope of a visual inspection, the buyer should seek specialty expertise in the specific area in question.

If questions remain that could be answered by the seller, ask them in writing. All questions and answers should be in writing, lest they later be misunderstood or denied.

Many would say that the key to life is the right answers. A person has a question in mind and goes about the task of obtaining the correct answer to their question. In time, the right answer is found. How is it then that we sometimes get to the correct answer, but are left with a bad outcome? The answer is that we asked the wrong question!

The challenge is really to ask the right questions! You see, if we have the wrong questions, and get to the correct answer, we falsely believe that a positive outcome will follow. Not so! We must have the correct answer to the correct question to be assured of a positive outcome.

Please, in home inspections as in all areas of life, take the time to first find the correct questions. When confronted with a question that is of deep and sincere concern to the buyer, but in reality is of no import or significance to making an objective decision about the home, it is the responsibility of the inspector to bring the question to correctness. Then correct answers will follow close behind.

Take Me to Your Assassin

The home inspection profession is truly beginning to mature. From its early beginnings with people from the trades being sought to "give it a look" to today's sophisticated use of computers, infrared technology, borescopes, moisture meters, and digital reports complete with color photographs and instantaneous online references, home inspectors are here to stay.

Those buyers, sellers, and real estate professionals who take the time to learn to choose their inspector wisely will be well rewarded with the information needed to close the deal in a manner that will be comfortable, informative, and profitable. They will come to know and respect the Deal Closer.

Those who shun sound, objective advice, or those who seek the blind inspector, or those who choose and refer based on cheapest price, will come to know the Deal Killer.

Always remember, bad news doesn't taste better with time, it only continues to sour. A done deal gone sour will make you wish you had met the Contract Assassin!

CPSIA information can be obtained at www.ICGtesting.com
Printed in the USA
LVOW11s1552290715

448106LV00024B/1563/P